*Mike ha[...]t makes this
topic see[...] a positive
approach to parenting and discipline, in an area of
family life where this can be a challenge.*

—Margarita Sims,
MT-BC (Music Therapist-Board Certified),
Parent

*I smiled the whole time I was reading the chapter
on single parenting. I found myself nodding in
agreement with what Mike was saying. He offers
excellent advice on the eternal "Mommy does it one
way and Daddy does it the other" problem. This will
be on my "recommended reading" list.*

—Barbara Spade, Parent,
International VP of Community Relations,
Parents Without Partners, Inc.

*Mike's unique perspective and understanding of this
misunderstood behavioral problem should be
required reading for teachers and parents alike. His
solutions are on target; his down-to-earth tone
and humor will make you want to read this book.*

—Mick Friedberg, M.S.,
Psychologist,
Salinas School District in California

*Organize Your Children, Spouse, and Home*

# STOP Clutter FROM Wrecking Your Family

*By*

## MIKE NELSON

New Page Books
A Division of The Career Press, Inc.
Franklin Lakes, NJ

STOP CLUTTER FROM WRECKING YOUR FAMILY
EDITED BY CLAYTON W. LEADBETTER
TYPESET BY EILEEN DOW MUNSON
Cover design by DesignConcept
Cover inset illustration by Getty Images/Peter Paul Connolly
Printed in the U.S.A. by Book-mart Press

To order this title, please call toll-free 1-800-CAREER-1 (NJ and Canada: 201-848-0310) to order using VISA or MasterCard, or for further information on books from Career Press.

The Career Press, Inc., 3 Tice Road, PO Box 687,
Franklin Lakes, NJ 07417
**www.careerpress.com**
**www.newpagebooks.com**

**Library of Congress Cataloging-in-Publication Data**

Nelson, Mexico Mike, 1950-
  Stop clutter from wrecking your family : organize your children, spouse, and home / by Mike Nelson.
    p. cm.
  Includes bibliographical references and index.
  ISBN 1-56414-718-5 (paper)
    1. Storage in the home. 2. House cleaning. 3. Behavior modification.  I. Title.

TX309.N45 2004
640—dc22

2003058193

*To my mother and father,*
*who did the best they could*
*with what they had to work with.*

## Acknowledgments

Thanks to all those who helped shape this book. So many kind people gave me assistance that it would be impossible to thank them all.

Thanks to the countless parents and children of clutterers who anonymously shared their stories and examples of what worked and didn't work in their families. I would like to thank those who attended Clutterless Recovery Groups meetings and shared their stories and checked my ideas with their real-world experiences.

Several teachers across the country provided valuable insights (mostly asking not to be credited) and verified my chapters relating to learning. Lee Boyd Montgomery, of Santa Fe, New Mexico, offered succinct evaluations on practical ways to deal with cluttering kids. Karen Wiggins, Ph.D., of Galveston Independent School District (GISD), provided real-world scenarios. Frederika Kotin, Ph.D., also with GISD, had tremendous insight and provided strategies that work, especially with troublesome teens. Rick Collett, a teacher of wide experience, was invaluable.

Special thanks goes to Margarita Simms, MT-BC, a parent and music therapist who reviewed, revised, and contributed her practical knowledge to every aspect of the book.

Thanks to: Michael J. Bradley, Ed.D., author of *Yes, Your Teen Is Crazy!,* who generously shared his time in interviews, and Dr. Terrence Early, M.D., who added several new perspectives, especially on AD/HD. Thanks also to his children who helped with the teenage and preteen perspectives on what parents can do.

Many therapists, who are also parents, helped enormously with the psychological recommendations. Thanks especially to Kim Arrington Cooper, M.Ed., a family therapist and neurobehavioral psychometrist.

Several dozen parents reviewed my strategies and contributed their own. Those who wanted to be mentioned include: Dan and Diane McNey, and Trudy, Charna, and Ronnie Graber.

And, of course, the greatest acknowledgement of all goes to my mother, Aurelie Nelson, and my father, Meredith Nelson, who gave me the confidence and encouragement that I could become a writer in the first place.

# Conventions Used in This Book

Cluttering is neither a male or female trait, so I've intermittently swapped *he*, *him*, and *his* with *she*, *her*, and *hers*. Repeating *husband* or *wife* seemed awkward, so I alternately inserted *partner* a number of times to avoid sexism.

Because many readers will have more than one child (lucky you!), I've used the word *children* wherever possible. The major exception to this is in the chapter about AD/HD children, when it's less likely that you'll have two with this disorder. Sometimes, to make a lesson pertinent, I had to say *child*, *him*, or *her*.

I purposely did not break the general headings into specific age groups, except for teens, because many parents will have children of different ages and the big picture is the same. The reasons for cluttering are universal, for the most part. So are the methods to overcome it, with obvious allowances for age differences. Within the chapters, I've indicated how to modify specific techniques for different age groups.

I coined a phrase, "not-cluttering," to indicate a way of life that's free from clutter. Not-cluttering is more important than decluttering.

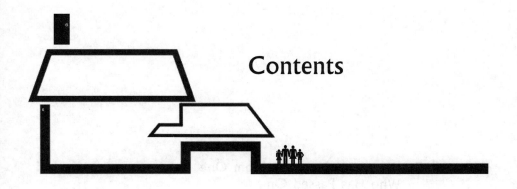

# Contents

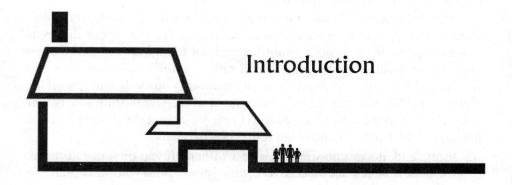

# Introduction

People are more important than things. Balance is the key. Relieving stress about cluttering is the way.

This book is not just about decluttering. It's about balance. A cluttered household is an unbalanced household. But so is a home where unreasonable expectations of neatness cause discord. If clutter or disorganization is causing stress in your family, the answers to relieving it are here. The answers aren't cut and dried. "Do this and your kid's sock drawers will stay neat and tidy. Do that and your husband will be able to find his keys." Those are the symptoms. We're going to go deeper than that. (But yes, we'll also help keyless spouses and sockless children get organized.)

Cluttering is a behavior. Clutter is a symptom. To change a behavior, you've got to treat the causes, not the symptoms, using practical and psychological tools. Until now, you've concentrated on the stuff, better organizing techniques, and finding the right organizing tools to make the messes go away. Those things are valuable, but they're like mowing the weeds in your lawn. Mow them, and the lawn will look good for a few weeks; uproot them, and they'll stay gone. We're gong to stop mowing and start uprooting.

I know how clutter can wreck family life. I've been there. I counsel people whose families are in a constant state of turmoil because of someone's cluttering. Both clutterers and non-clutterers have broken down and cried because of the stress clutter causes in their relationships. The stuff has come between them and those they love. The child who clutters, the partner who imprisons the family in a cluttered home, the teen who's ashamed to invite her friends over are my family. You are my family. Together, we will solve this challenge.

Most "organizing" books are written by well-meaning people who aren't cluttered for people who are cluttered. In many ways, they speak different languages. I've lived in both countries and am bilingual (he said with an appropriately self-effacing grin). I can talk "clutter" with clutterers and translate that so non-clutterers can understand. Your kids and grandkids clutter for different reasons. So does your spouse. The bottom line is that cluttering is about control. Learning to live a not-cluttering lifestyle is about harnessing that control and using it in a positive sense.

In the end, it's not how much or how little stuff you or your kids have, or how neat it is. It's about how you, your spouse, and your kids relate to each other and how to keep material things from coming between you.

May you find comfort and solutions here. May you find peace.

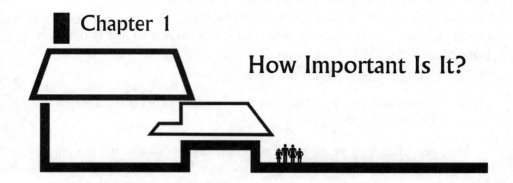

# Chapter 1

## How Important Is It?

*My cluttering goes back to my childhood, I guess. Maybe that is something you should address in your new book—that parents need to get a grip on their child's cluttering ASAP. Especially because there are other issues underneath it! I wish my parents had done something back then. Maybe I wouldn't be in the mess (literally) that I am in today.*

*I remember that I used to be a very neat and organized child. I had a place for everything and my room was always perfect. Spotless! I even dusted it weekly. Well, my mother was abusive and I became depressed, and I am not sure when it was exactly, but my clutter first became apparent around that time (perhaps around age 12 or 13). Instead of being neat as a pin, I began piling papers and books and magazines and catalogs on my bed—anything at all. Clothes were thrown on the floor. Once it began, no one put a stop to it.*

—Janine,
a recovering clutterer

Kids' messiness a constant battle? Spouse's clutter causing friction in your relationship? The solutions are here, but the problem isn't what you think. Stuff isn't the problem. Organizing techniques alone aren't the answer. Understanding is the key. Loving communication is the way. Hope is what this book is all about. It's about living a happier, less stressful life—not just having a neater home. It's about balance.

There's a lot of psychology here, but it boils down to just two simple principles:

1. Kids and adults clutter for a reason.

2. They clutter because they get rewarded, negatively or positively, for doing it.

Aw, gee, cluttering may be serious, but a key element to overcoming it is to lighten up, literally and figuratively. While it may not rival the Macarena in popularity, you and your family will be doing the "clutter dance" to celebrate your successes, having "treasure hunts," and awarding poker chips as rewards. Hugs and kisses are mandatory. Humor is the best medicine and the best teacher.

How many clutterers does it take to change a lightbulb?

*None. They have dozens of lightbulbs, but can't find them.*

The stories in this book are true; only the names have been changed to protect the cluttered. Dozens of clutterers shared their childhood memories with you and me, under the condition of anonymity. No clutterers were harmed in the making of this book.

## This Is a Guidebook

I'm just a guide on your journey to understanding cluttering and applying what you know to a behavior you don't understand. You're the expert on your family dynamics. There aren't a lot of "shoulds" and "ought tos" here. There's no guilt. There are a lot of suggestions of what has worked in families such as yours. Take what you need and leave the rest.

Cluttering behavior and habits are family issues. How your kids deal with their stuff may reflect what's going on within your family or within themselves. Or, they could just need a little guidance on what to do and why it's important. Whatever the reasons, you'll learn solutions that work for children and adults, not just bandages of organizing tips.

## The Lone Ranger to the Rescue

Heck, sometimes decluttering can result in some great family stories. Kids love to play make-believe and sometimes they'll pretend themselves into a decluttering project. Join in with them. Whenever all this "dealing with the issue" stuff gets too intense, remember that there's a lighter side to everything. Stay on the sunny side of the street!

"I'm one of those people who'll wait until the last moment to finish a project. Then, just as it looks as if I couldn't possibly have enough time to complete it, I'll burst on the scene with a fresh load of energy and get the job done in record time. It's as if I'm trying to be the Lone Ranger who prances in on his high white horse and saves the day just in the nick of time.

"This high-tension approach to getting things done has its roots in one of my earliest childhood memories. It involves a method my mom used to encourage us—my brother and sister and I—to pick up our toys. Mom would leave the playroom and we would see if we could clean it up by the time she got back. We'd work ourselves up into a frenzy trying to get everything in place. If we managed to get it cleaned up in time, she'd let us know by being very theatrical. After giving the room a thorough once-over with her eyes, she'd open them widely and exclaim, 'I have NEVER seen ANYTHING like this! I think I'm going to FAINT!' Then she'd close her eyes and crumple like a rag doll onto a nearby mattress. The three of us would laugh and cheer. We felt strong and powerful, like gnomes in a storybook who had just felled the mighty giant."

—Elizabeth,
a recovering clutterer

## Imitation or Rebellion?

Are your kids imitating (or rebelling against) you with their cluttering? Are you imitating (or rebelling against) your own parents with your standards of neatness?

You may have to change some of your own ways of dealing with the things in your life. It's easier to teach our children to learn how to not-clutter than it is for our spouses (or ourselves) to change. The tools here have been tested in real, live homes with real, live clutterers—both children and adults. The only experts on the clutter in your home are you and the clutterer who made it. Learning how to organize will help, but learning to want to not-clutter is the key.

Learning how not to be messy, or not-clutter, may not rank as high as potty training in helping your child fit into society (though the parallels are obvious), but it's right up there with learning to say "please" and "thank you." Some of the traits that learning to not-clutter will reinforce are far more important than getting rid of stuff or just having a neat house.

### Lifestyle Traits Learned From Decluttering

- Respect for others.
- Decision-making.
- Concern for those less fortunate.
- Increased self-esteem.
- Decreased anxiety at home, school, and in adulthood.
- Combating depression.
- Taking responsibility for one's actions.
- Better study habits.
- Acceptance of ourselves and what we need.
- Gratitude for what we do have.
- Respect for property.
- A sense of balance in having what we need and want, and not letting those things we neither need nor want vying for our attention.

The solutions come from understanding the reasons people—adults and children—hang on to their stuff. They aren't just learning to make neat "homes" for stuff in brightly colored containers or following rigid rules about "keeping neat."

Rules are fine and necessary for a household to run. Structure is needed (and psychologists tell us actually wanted) by children and teens. Rules help families function smoothly. But understanding why kids and adults make messes is a far more powerful tool for permanently changing cluttering behavior. Ever had a child ask, "Why?" when you told her to pick something up or put it away? Now you'll be able (most of the time anyway) to come up with something better than, "Because I said so, that's why." I doubt I'll ever rank up with Dr. Spock, but if you want to say, "Because Mike Nelson said so, that's why," go ahead. Heck, to a 5-year-old, that might mean something.

## This Is a Journey, Not a Trip

If you're looking for a quick fix, you might as well put this book down now. Quick fixes don't last. If those quick fixes worked, you wouldn't be looking here for a new solution. I promise you that once you learn the "why" of cluttering, you can apply the "how to." You get both here. You need both to do any permanent good. If you want to make a real difference in your children's lives, repair your marriage, have a happier home, and are willing to learn a new paradigm, then welcome. Let's begin the journey.

### Lighten Up

First of all, though, lighten up. Don't expect spic-and-span perfection from your kids. And don't expect them to become your housekeepers or to take care of the entire family's clutter. Impose too strict a neatening regimen on your children now, and many of them will flip 180 degrees in adulthood and become clutterers as adults. I've heard this story way too often from attendees at Clutterless Recovery Group meetings.

Dr. Michael Bradley, Ed.D., a psychologist who specializes in teens and author of *Yes, Your Teen Is Crazy!* and *Yes, Your Parents Are Crazy*, told me in an interview that how you approach neatness in your family can make a big difference later on:

> "Taking it [neatness] to an extreme and taking care of the house is too heavy. Throttle back your expectations. If the parent can't do

it, it is unfair. Those kids grow up hating being neat. They often rebel against relationships because the emotional demands of childhood were too great to maintain an entire house."

## This Book Is All About Making Your Life Easier—Not Harder

Not-cluttering and decluttering are like schoolwork or athletics. Some kids are naturally adept and will be neat all by themselves. Most kids will want to be uncluttered, if only to please you when they are very young, but have to work at it. And a few won't want to and just plain won't do it. This book is designed to make your life as a parent easier, not to add any additional stress or yet another set of goals to be the "perfect" parent. There isn't such a thing. Being a parent is a tough, demanding art, not a science. The rewards are worth it, which is why otherwise sane adults volunteer for 18 years of hard labor. Maybe Pete Seeger got it right when he said, "We do it for the high wages…kisses."

It's hard to know the "right" way to parent. Read 20 books on parenting, and you'll get 14 different opinions on the best way to raise your children. Dr. Benjamin Spock said simply, "Don't be overawed by what the experts say…the natural loving care that kindly parents give their children is a hundred times more important…."

Read all you can, take expert advice under advisement, and then incorporate that into your own understanding of yourself and your children. My opinions and those of the professionals presented here are just that—opinions. Real experts have also been interviewed—moms and dads, kids, adult children, grandmothers and grandfathers. Some of what you read here will rub you the wrong way. Good. That either means it doesn't apply to your family, or that I struck a chord about something you don't want to deal with. Some of you will feel validated for thinking the way you already do. Good. A thinking parent is a better parent. A thinking kid is a better kid. People are just better when they think instead of just react.

## The Goal Is to Improve Your Kid's Self-Esteem

My goal here is to offer you some tools to take back your time, help you teach your children ways to feel better about themselves that will carry over into adulthood, and bring peace to your family. But it's going to take work on your part. It's going to take parenting and relationship-building. It's going to take understanding and loving. And sometimes it will take discipline.

Please note that I didn't say "punishment." Discipline is a positive experience. Punishment is negative. When you discipline a child, you teach him the consequences for his actions, but provide him with insight so as not to repeat the behavior. When you punish a child, you perform negative reinforcement of the behavior that is self-defeating and frustrating. Kids need attention. If they get more attention from their negative behavior, they'll keep doing the negative behavior. If they get attention from positive behavior, that will be their preferred method. That's behavioral psychology 101. It's true, proven by rodents and people all over the world.

Yelling, hitting, and making ultimatums all punish a child. Taking away privileges and items, giving time-outs, and cutting back allowances are forms of discipline. They focus the penalty on the action, not the child. Admittedly time-outs won't work with your spouse, but there are better ways to deal with a cluttering spouse than yelling, hitting, nagging, and ultimatums.

## Understanding Behaviors Enables Us to Change Them, Not Use Them as Excuses

Understanding a behavior doesn't mean making excuses for it. Your children may clutter just because they don't know how not to. They may just be messy because they never thought of it as a problem. And some kids are just messy.

There could be deeper psychological reasons for the behavior, such as a reaction to anxiety, change in schools, divorce, death of a family member or friend, and many other reasons. Yes, learn to understand that the behavior has a reason; try to treat the reason, not punish the person. Sometimes all you can do is acknowledge the reason and then explain that cluttering isn't the way to deal with it. Sometimes you have to be a parent and insist that rooms get cleaned up, toys and books get put away, and so on. Sometimes you have to take away a privilege to get your children to do something they don't want to do.

It's easier to teach your child how to not-clutter than it is for your spouse to learn to declutter. They've had more practice at it and have formed more deeply ingrained habits. Fortunately, one of the motivators that really works for adult clutterers is that changing one's cluttering habits is part of good parenting. Your kids learn from you. They imitate you. The biggest thing you can do to help them learn to live clutter-free lives is to learn to declutter yourself.

## You're Already a Good Parent

You're a good parent. It's tough enough to be a parent without some-body telling you one more thing you should do. I'm not real big into "shoulds." "Want tos" work better. If you *want to* change something, you're more likely to do it than if you *should* do something. Your kids are no different. You know more about raising your own children than any psychiatrist, teacher, counselor, or author could ever know. All I can do is to offer suggestions that have worked for other parents.

You do the best you can for your children. You make sacrifices on all levels, from financial to personal, to provide them with love, a roof over their heads, good food, and a safe environment. No matter what your so-cioeconomic level, you spend your money on things to make your children happy. Especially if you came from a financially distressed background (as did I), you may have vowed that your children would never want for any-thing. You do this out of love. There's nothing wrong with a little selfish motive mixed in. If your children have enough toys and games to occupy themselves, you might get a little more quiet time that you deserve.

How well has that worked? Is your quiet time shorter than the time you spend picking up those toys, clothes, games, or trying to convince your kids to pick them up? What's wrong with this picture?

## Do You Have a Thief in the House?

Cluttering is a thief. Has your familial peace and tranquility been shat-tered by confrontations with your children about leaving a mess in the liv-ing room? Do you spend too much time pleading, reasoning, and finally shouting at them to clean up their rooms or put their things away? Clutter-ing has stolen precious time and tranquility from you and your family. We're going to change that. You do remember what tranquility is, don't you?

### Things Don't Equal Happiness

Buying things does not buy happiness. Everything has a price beyond monetary cost. More things means more time spent taking care of them. Whether it's the latest popular toy or computer game for your children or a larger house for your family, things don't live up to their promise of providing more happiness or free time. Don't worry, I'm not a minimalist, a communist, or any other kind of "ist." I like things too. There's nothing morally wrong with having possessions. It's not about morality. It's about understanding the true cost of what we buy for our children and ourselves.

Let's put cluttering into a new paradigm. Cluttering isn't about stuff. It's about how we relate to our stuff, or what our stuff represents.

As a cluttering adult, you or your spouse may already be aware that just knowing how to organize and how to follow systems and rules that seem to work for your uncluttered friends doesn't work for you. If it was that simple, you would have decluttered and stayed that way long ago. There are many books written on "how to" declutter. This one is about "how to change and not want to clutter."

## Cluttering Is a Habit. Not-Cluttering Is a Habit

Children like routine. It gives structure to their lives. It makes them feel secure. Even teenagers, according to psychologists, want routine in their family lives, no matter how much they grouse about it. Grousing is just part of being a teen. By teaching your children not-cluttering habits and routines, you'll give them a sense of self-discipline and enhance their self-esteem. It'll be easier to teach your children to live uncluttered lives than it will be to change your spouse's cluttering behavior, but we're going to do that too. On the most basic level, cluttering is a habit. Not-cluttering is also a habit. Forming habits in childhood are easier than breaking them as adults.

Establishing routines can help to overcome cluttering tremendously. It can also make a parent's life easier. The routine of setting a bedtime and sticking to it is often a source of frustration and disharmony in a family. You'll learn how that's related to cluttering behavior and how to implement routines in a way that almost makes it easy. Heck, It would be disingenuous of me if I said getting children to bed or to do anything else is always going to be easy. But, hey, if we can make something easy 80 percent of the time, instead of 20 percent of the time, wouldn't that be great? (I made those statistics up—who can really quantify something like that? But I guarantee you, it will feel like a huge improvement.)

> "Your idea to equate clutter maintenance with a bedtime routine is good. One of the routines we have in our home is a 'cleanup song' (borrowed from Barney) that really motivates the kids. Or we will race each other to clean up, or pick up all items of one color or category first, and so on. Those little games seem to help."
>
> —Margarita, mother of two

## Special Challenges for Special Situations

You or your children may have been relatively neat, then started cluttering. This is probably a reaction to a major change in your lives, the loss of a job, an ended relationship, divorce, or the loss of a family member or friend. Take heart. These life traumas can be overcome and so can the cluttering associated with them. You'll appreciate Chapter 13.

### Single Parents

One of the biggest challenges for a single parent is that the loss of a partner has disrupted the routines of their children. You may have had to move. Your economic circumstances may be tighter. Schools get changed. Friends are lost. These changes in routine are difficult for children (*and* adults—your reactions to these life-changing events are important too).

As a single working mom or dad, you just don't have enough time to pick up after your children. You probably don't even have time to pick up after yourself the way you'd like. Guess what? Your children don't care if you live in a *House Beautiful* home. You don't have to try to live up to impossible standards of neatness for yourself or your children. We'll learn to determine realistic standards that both you and your children can agree to maintain. Making them partners will make your family stronger.

See the previous caveat about lightening up. It's common for children to be treated like adults in one-parent families. They aren't. They're kids. Children should have responsibilities, but only as much as they can handle and still be childlike.

A cluttering pitfall into which separated parents often fall is that they want to buy their children more things to replace the time they can't give them. One isn't a substitute for the other.

The custodial parent and the other parent may have different attitudes about cluttering. This can be used to help your kids understand how important the issue of cluttering is, but it's also not worth a battle. See Chapter 11 for effective ways to deal with this situation.

## Cluttering Has Psychological Roots

Cluttering in adults and children is tied up with emotions such as fear, insecurity, wanting to shut people out of our lives, anxiety, and depression. Mix in a smattering of behaviors that resemble obsessive-compulsive disorder (OCD) and attention deficit hyperactivity disorder (AD/HD), and you've got a tough nut to crack.

Cluttering in childhood can have some of those elements, but don't freak out. Your kids don't have to enter therapy to learn to keep their rooms neat. You don't need an M.D. or a Ph.D. to understand what's going on. If you understand what's behind their behavior, you'll know how to change it. Sometimes just teaching not-cluttering behaviors can nip the problem in the bud. Rewarding children for not-cluttering can reinforce this behavior in a positive way. Teaching them pride of ownership and respect for themselves can manifest in their living less cluttered lives.

Children may use cluttering behaviors to express their independence. You want an independent child (well, sometimes), because an independent child will grow into an independent adult. And an independent child will take less of your time, because she will do things on her own without being reminded by you.

### Cluttering Is Paradoxical

Cluttering is a conundrum. Independence is "positive." Being messy is "negative." The key is to channel this "negative" expression of self into more positive outlets.

Children may clutter because they're anxious or depressed. They may feel so overwhelmed with life that it spills over into their rooms and school-work.

Control and rebellion are usually big factors in cluttering. Children can't control much that's going on in their lives. But they can control their rooms. They may feel that keeping it neat is something their parents want, not something they want. By expressing control over their mess, they assert themselves and rebel against their parents indirectly. This can be overcome by teaching them to value their space and possessions. When you teach them that keeping things messy is really controlling them, they'll value neatness as their expression of control.

## In Conclusion

Let's get started on this journey to understanding and changing your children's, spouse's, and maybe even your own cluttering behavior. We aren't just going to learn how to make "homes" for things, impose "systems," or believe that going to the local "Clutter-Solutions Depot" and getting the right boxes, bins, and containers is going to solve this problem. I say "we," because (in case you skipped the introduction and missed my eloquent preamble) for the next couple of hundred pages, you are my family. We're going to make that mean old Clutter Monster more like the Cookie Monster—big, but not intimidating. We'll teach your children some real values that will serve them in good stead for the rest of their lives, and take a lot of stress out of your home. Chances are, we'll have a chuckle or two doing it. Cluttering is serious, but we don't have to be.

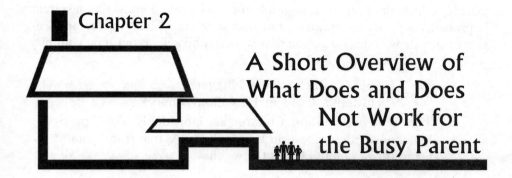

## Chapter 2

# A Short Overview of What Does and Does Not Work for the Busy Parent

*A Cherokee elder was teaching his grandchildren about life. He said to them,"A fight is going on inside me. It is a terrible fight, and it is between two wolves. One wolf represents fear, anger, envy, sorrow, regret, greed, arrogance, self-pity, guilt, resentment, inferiority, lies, false pride, superiority, and ego. The other wolf stands for joy, peace, love, hope, sharing, serenity, humility, kindness, benevolence, friendship, empathy, generosity, truth, compassion, and faith. This same fight is going on inside you, and inside every other person, too."*

*They thought about it for a minute and then one child asked his grandfather, "Which wolf will win?"*

*The old Cherokee simply replied,"The one you feed."*

—Anonymous

When the wolves are at your door, this chapter can help you refocus. It's a short overview that you can come back to when you just need an idea about how to stay on track. It's at the beginning of the book, so you'll get some immediate, bite-sized ideas of what this book is all about. There are no immediate, simple solutions to cluttering, but brief ideas such as this can help you keep your focus.

I know it's hard to find time to read when you've got children demanding your attention (oops, I know the little darlings never *demand*; perhaps they just ask insistently), a job to go to, a house to take care of, and, oh yes, possibly a little time for being an adult and having fun. I know that last item is probably a pretty low priority, but with luck and, I believe, the application of the ideas in this book, you may someday be able to put it on your list.

### Decluttering Nuggets
### (There's Gold in Here Somewhere)

1. There is no *one* solution. Children are individuals. You'll probably choose one suggestion from column A, one from column B, and throw column C out the window.

2. You are the expert. I am only the guide.

3. Children learn by imitation. Are they imitating you when they clutter? If so, let's learn how to change your behavior as you teach them to change theirs. Your whole family will benefit.

4. Cluttering is a symptom. It is not a cause.

5. What works for one child may not work or may work differently for another. One size does *not* fit all.

6. What worked at age 4 won't necessarily work later. Modify decluttering strategies as your children grow.

7. More important than decluttering or neatness are the values that being neat teaches your children.

8. Please remember that you aren't just teaching neatness. You're teaching them to live freer, more productive lives that show respect for other people. People are always more important than things.

9. A child who learns to not-clutter and to organize will do better in school and life. That's the big picture. That's what you're trying to teach. That's why it's such a big deal.

10. If you or your spouse are clutterers, your children may see little reason not to be. On the other hand (there are always other hands), some of your children will be neat just to show that they are individuals. While this may seem like a perfect situation, when they grow up, they're likely to turn into clutterers

because the focal point for their rebellion is gone. It's a better solution to work on your own cluttering habits.

11. Your children can be your best allies in your own war against cluttering.

12. If your children are the neatest, most organized kids on the block, but selfish, then their relationship to things is still skewed.

13. Merely organizing is not the goal. Healthy relationships are the goals. You want your children to understand how their cluttering affects them and others. Most importantly, you wish to teach them to understand how stuff is useful, but that it is only stuff. More or better possessions do not define them as people; fewer possessions do not make them any less of a person than the rich kid with a room full of toys, games, dolls, or anything else.

14. Nagging may work for the short term. But the cost, in terms of additional stress to you and your children, make it very inefficient. Rewarding acceptable behavior works a lot better. This is a long-term solution that teaches children they can get more attention by following the rules than by rebelling.

15. Cluttering causes stress. Stress causes anxiety. No one is at his best when anxious.

16. Cluttering may be an expression of bigger things going on with your children. Cluttering is often a manifestation of AD/HD, anxiety, depression, or rebellion. Learn to treat the causes, not the symptoms.

17. Not-cluttering is more important and easier than decluttering.

18. Decluttering is boring. Fortunately, there are ways to bring some excitement into it.

19. If decluttering or not-cluttering is seen as a chore, it's less likely to be done. Learn to make it a game.

20. Routines work. Make decluttering part of playing, studying, and being part of the family—part of the routine of living, such as going to bed at a certain hour.

21. Rigidity and inflexibility work only to a point. Be too rigid and your children will use their cluttering as a weapon to rebel against you.

22. Conflict is a necessary part of living. Listen to your children when they say or demonstrate that they don't want to declutter. Maybe they have a better idea. Maybe they aren't motivated to do it anymore. Maybe some modifications in your rules will ease the conflict and get the results you want.

23. In the final analysis, you are the parent. You make the decisions based on your knowledge of your children and your vision for your children. Mother and Father do know best. None of the experts on parenting live with *your* children—you do.

24. Sometimes nothing works.

25. Sometimes you'll resort to ordering your children to "pick things up, or else." "Or else" is a vague, scary concept. If you occasionally use fear as a motivator, you haven't failed as a parent. You're just being human. Everyone—parents *and* children—gets frustrated.

26. Occasionally, everyone is cluttered. Temporary setbacks do not undo months of successes. Accept yours and your children's backsliding as part of the process.

27. No one is a perfect child or parent. But we are all perfect expressions of who we are.

28. I hate to say it, but decluttering or not-cluttering is not the most important thing in life. If your children are relatively well adjusted, happy, and drug-free, have "good" friends, aren't selfish, and are doing well at school, then evaluate how much stress cluttering is causing in your family. If they're just a little cluttered, don't make it into a big deal that causes a fight.

## Changing Habits Isn't Just for Nuns

"One day, when I was 13, my mother got really upset with me for the way I kept my bathroom. I never cleaned the tub and it had a huge ring around it. 'Don't you even know how to clean your tub?' she screamed. In fact, I didn't. I'd never been taught how to do even this basic chore."

—Edith,
a recovering clutterer

Cluttering is a habit. Not-cluttering is a habit. Sometimes kids are messy just because they haven't been taught not to be. It's far more difficult to declutter than to not-clutter in the first place. Everyone knows that, logically. Everyone who clutters also knows it is easier said than done. You've probably tried setting down rules about where stuff goes and bought a lot of pretty containers to put neatly organized stuff into. It hasn't worked has it? Don't blame yourself. It's not because you didn't try, or because you aren't a good parent. It's because the right motivation wasn't there. You hadn't been taught to approach this problem from the inside. There is real hope that we can change the habits of our children and keep them from making some of the messes in the first place.

To borrow a line from physics, every cluttering habit has an equal and opposite not-cluttering habit. Remember, the easiest reward for adopting not-cluttering habits is to acknowledge the preferred behavior with a thank-you or a hug.

"In some families I've worked with, the kids were shocked when momma said 'thank you' to acknowledge good behavior."

—Kim Arrington Cooper, M.Ed.,
marriage and family counselor

Later on, we'll get into reward systems in detail. The chart on page 30 is a synopsis of how those rewards can be applied to specific cluttering issues. While this is about negative cluttering habits, don't forget to reward their opposites—not-cluttering habits.

For Everything, There Is an Opposite

| Cluttering Habit | Not-Cluttering Habit | How To Change—Positive Method | How To Change—Discipline |
|---|---|---|---|
| Leaving toys out. | Putting toys away at end of play. | Playtime isn't over until toys are put up. Give your children a 10-minute warning that it's time to pick up. | Toys that are left out get put into a "penalty box" until the end of the week. |
| Throwing clothes on floor. | Putting dirty clothes in hamper. | Get a clothes basket or hamper without a top to make it easier. | Clothes on the floor are put away for a week. |
| Not making bed. | Making bed every morning. | Get started on the day 15 minutes early, with the understanding that making the bed is the reason. Make a game of it. If bed can be made in five minutes, give child the extra time to sleep in. | You can't put the bed into "time-out," but you can deduct points from the not-cluttering score. |
| Misplacing schoolwork. | Having schoolwork ready to go at the end of the night. | Make a place for backpack to "live" for the evening. Study time isn't done until books are packed and ready to go. Give a 15-minute warning. | This might sound harsh, but if your child has to go to school without some books once or twice, he'll learn that the consequences outweigh the inaction. |
| Leaving a mess in the kitchen. | Cleaning up, putting back. | Point out how easy it is to find treats when they are in the same place. | Progressively hide, or don't buy items left out. "I thought you didn't like them because you don't appreciate them." |
| Losing portable phone, cell phone. | Putting them up. | Interrupt child when doing something she likes and asking her to find the phone. | Take away phone privileges for a day for each offense. |
| Losing TV remote. | Putting it up. | See above. | Take away TV privileges for an hour for each offense. |

You'll think of more specific things that apply to your own home. The principle is the same for everything. Try the positive method first. If that doesn't work, try the discipline method. One way or another, your kids will learn that for everything they do, there's a trade-off.

## Some Practical Suggestions That Work for Most Kids From Pre-K to Preteen

Of all the parents, counselors, and child psychiatrists I interviewed, Trudy, a mother of six children, including a set of twins, boiled down the best simple solutions for the "how-to" part of keeping her kids decluttered:

"Put as much as you can into clear containers. Toy boxes don't cut it. If kids can't see what's in a box, they'll take everything out. Shoebox-size works best, depending on the size of the contents. Toy cars go in one. Dishes go in another. Building pieces live in a bucket. The Container Store is my best friend.

"Have wire shelves in each room. Boxes can stack neatly on a shelf. Bigger items such as dollhouses can sit on top or on the floor.

"Make it a game. Whoever can clean the fastest wins. Make rewards small and projects attainable. Go to the park. Have ice cream. Have friends over.

"Kids' attitude towards being cluttered change as they grow older. Some are organized and some not. The only one who is organized now is the oldest (seventh grade), but not when he was little. Now he picks up without my telling him."

## What Hasn't Worked in Trudy's Home

"Telling the kids to stay in their room until it's clean hasn't worked. They would stay there for two or three days.

"Just telling them, 'go and clean your room' has not worked either. They have a natural resistance to cleaning, seeing it as a dreaded chore and avoiding it as much as possible. One of them said, 'I'd rather go to the dentist and have my teeth pulled.' It is better to call it something else, such as 'getting your room ready for your friends to come over.'

"Follow that up with specific recommendations, such as making the bed, hanging up clothes, and getting the desk cleared off to make it easier to study. You have to be really specific about what you want done. They may pick up one or two pieces of clothing from a pile on the floor and consider the job done.

"Withholding their allowances for not picking up has not proven effective."

## There You Have It

This book will be unlike any other you may have read about cluttering or organization. I've taken a holistic approach, combining simple, practical steps, unconventional ideas taken from real-life clutterers and their families, and psychiatric concepts. When you put it all together, you'll see that cluttering is a behavior that can't be solved with just one approach. It takes a village to raise a child, and it takes various approaches to overcome cluttering. Let's go!

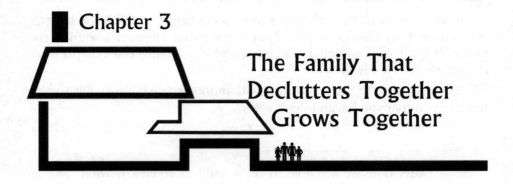

# Chapter 3

## The Family That Declutters Together Grows Together

*You are right on stating that picking up after your kids sets up that expectation. Mike, I am embarrassed to say this was true as I was growing up. I had no idea I should have been responsible for cleaning anything other than my room. Explaining the difference between housework and decluttering (I have trouble with both) is an important concept to learn.*

—Jane, a mom,
a clutterer,
and a therapist

Cluttering isn't just the kids' problem. It's the whole family's. So are the solutions. The more parents, psychiatric professionals, and teachers I interviewed, the more different answers I got about what works in real life. Some things work all of the time for some of the people and others work some of the time for some of the people. I guess Abe Lincoln was right. By the way, did you know he cluttered in his stovepipe hat? Yep, he kept lots of different items up there so he wouldn't forget them.

## Are You, Your Spouse, or Both Training Your Kids to Clutter?

If the parents clutter, it's going to be a challenge to teach the kids to not-clutter. They look up to you. They imitate you. They are also innately smart. If their role models haven't been able to figure out how to not-clutter, then how can they?

You may react to their cluttering with more disdain because it is something in you that you haven't dealt with.

"Every time we are able to see a little more clearly what our own issues are and where they come from, we have the possibility of choosing not to react in automatic and often destructive ways, and creating new and healthier possibilities instead."

—Myla and Jon Kabat-Zinn,
*Everyday Blessing: The Inner
Work of Mindful Parenting*

Don't give up hope! If you are a clutterer (as am I), you didn't get this way overnight and you aren't going to get decluttered in a few weeks, or even a few months. Slow and sure wins this race. You don't have to wait until you are "better" before teaching your children how to not-clutter, or involving the family in decluttering projects. Chances are, you've tried emergency decluttering sessions before, which didn't last. That's because you weren't taught the "why" behind the cluttering. You'll have to read the chapter on spouse clutter, and it wouldn't hurt to take a gander at my first clutter book, *Stop Clutter From Stealing Your Life*, to get a handle on adult cluttering.

Dr. Michael Bradley, author of *Yes, Your Teen Is Crazy!* and *Yes, Your Parents Are Crazy*, told me this, in response to what parents can do to teach children to learn to not-clutter, if they or their spouses are clutterers:

"It's like apparently not being able to stop smoking. The parents can say that they struggle with it and explain the emotional prices they pay. The parent is imperfect and is struggling to get better. Parents could talk about the pain involved—hopeless, helpless feelings they experience. Kids can relate to those feelings with their own feelings of hopelessness and helplessness when they've tried to do things that are hard for them, such as sports or classes they can't seem to get. Cluttering is a pseudo-addiction. Breaking that habit is very difficult."

If you or your spouse is a clutterer, please consider joining a support group such as Clutterless Recovery Groups (*www.clutterless.org*). You haven't been able to overcome this by yourself so far, have you? Support groups can help with most problems. Just knowing you aren't alone and being able to talk to others with similar situations helps tremendously.

# If the Parents Don't Clutter

You've got an easier row to hoe. Because your kids will be able to see that the messes they make are their own, they'll understand that they're doing something different than the rest of the family. The young ones will want to model themselves after you, and not-cluttering is already the model. All you'll need to do is teach them the techniques and reasons why not-cluttering is important. Please remember that, throughout this book, the reasons for doing or not doing something are more important than learning a lot of rules and tips. We want to change behavior on a basic level, not just the outside appearances.

# Strategies for Making Decluttering a Family Affair

The word *strategy* implies a war room. In a sense this is a war—a war against an enemy that's disrupting your family. Keep in mind that the enemy is the clutter, not the clutterers.

## Family Meetings

Have a family meeting. If your dining-room table is already cluttered, what a great place for a meeting! That is, unless you can't see the tops of the heads of the smaller family members sitting across from you. In that case, you may have to go somewhere else. With everyone present, talk about how the cluttered house affects the whole family. This can be a surprisingly emotional time. If the parent's are cluttered, a child may relate how ashamed she feels.

> "I spent most of my childhood being afraid of starting a dialog about the clutter. I didn't want to hurt my mom's feelings."
>
> —L.H.,
> daughter of a clutterer

## Don't Blame

Remember, this is a discussion, not a blame session. Even if only one kid or adult clutters, approach the problem as a family problem with family solutions. If the clutterer feels singled out (they already know they're the reason for the meeting), he will become defensive. When people become defensive, they stop listening. When people listen, they can negotiate and compromise.

## Changing Your Behavior

One thing you should make clear is that you were not put on this earth to pick up after everybody. If you are doing that now, you've set up the expectation that the children needn't worry about their clutter, because Mom or Dad will pick it up. Saying this and doing it are two different things, so you'll have to change your behavior (and learn to deal with your own frustration until the family begins to operate as a unit, not as individual commandos).

## Ongoing Change

This is not a one-time fix. Don't have such high standards of neatness that no one can live up to them. Don't expect everyone to agree to do something about the clutter and follow through forever. Cluttering is about control and limits. Overcoming it is about being willing to change.

## Using Pictures

Your children (or spouse) may say they don't see any clutter. Instead of shouting out, "Come on, are you blind as well as messy?" be ready with some examples. Pictures are worth a thousand words. Take some beforehand, not only to bolster your case, but because it will help everyone's efforts to know where the pictures came from and so they can gauge how far they've come. When people of any age look at their messes in real life, they don't seem as harsh as they do in photographs. If your house is pretty cluttered, you won't turn it into a feng shui masterpiece in a week. Post the pictures in prominent places so that when anyone gets discouraged (and they will), they'll have a baseline to keep them motivated.

## Decluttering and Housework

Differentiate between clutter and the regular housework that needs to be done to keep a family operating—chores such as washing dishes, sweeping, vacuuming, mopping, and so on. Most people don't get this right away, so I've included a section on explaining this important difference (see page 40).

## Making It Interesting

Acknowledge early on that you know getting rid of clutter is a boring task. But, because it has to be done, get some feedback on ways to make it more interesting. Here are some ideas:

▶ Think of decluttering as a treasure hunt. Keep a list of the most valuable items found. If there's money in the piles or in the pockets of jeans left in the living room, it belongs to the declutterer. Some people I know actually hide small bills in the clutter to get everyone started.

▶ Keep a list of the most "forgotten about" items found and have some sort of reward for the one who finds the most.

▶ Set a time for group decluttering, if that's feasible. Decluttering alone is tough. If that won't work, at least let your kids pick clutter buddies to work with. You can be a clutter buddy too. Just having another person around when you're doing this makes it easier.

- If adults get bored decluttering and their minds wander, that goes double for kids. The minimum time to declutter is 15 minutes a day. The maximum is around an hour for the stalwart. (I declutter in marathon sessions, because that works for me, but I don't recommend it for most people.) To keep interest up, keep a chart of decluttering time for everyone, with some sort of payoff for the one who spends the most. Staring at the clutter doesn't count. You have to actually do something. That's another good reason for a buddy. If keeps you honest.

- Because this is a family affair, have some sort of group reward for making progress. Make decluttering a game, especially with young ones.

- Make a big deal when anyone declutters anything, no matter how small an area. One family I know has a clutter dance they do when the young ones (or the mother) clears off an area.

- When anyone performs a not-cluttering activity, such as picking up their shoes from the living room, or recycling a newspaper or magazine, make just as big a deal over that. Sure, it will seem silly, but positive reinforcement wins every time.

- Teens probably will find the clutter dance silly, but they might respond to some kind of "clutter fight song."

- If you have a kid who's in a military frame of mind, he can dress in fatigues when decluttering. Make it a war game.

How small a thing is worth making a big deal about? Here's an e-mail from a recovering clutterer who has made tremendous progress in coming from a house where she couldn't have "play dates" for her children to invite others over, to a home where other children visit regularly:

> "I won't be at the Clutterless meeting this week, but you can tell the group I have good news and bad news. Good news: I threw out a can of burn relief spray with a February 1983 expiration date. Bad news: I had to talk myself

into doing so. I tried to convince myself that it had either deteriorated into uselessness or fermented into poison (unlikely). I still hesitated throwing it into the trash, but I did it! (applause)."

Your family will come up with a lot of interesting ideas. Nothing is out of bounds if it keeps them going. And what worked today may not work in a month. Serious kids will just as soon forgo the games. Use your own judgment. Whatever works, works.

## Rewards
People respond better to carrots than sticks. Ask everyone involved what sort of reward they might like for doing a good job. Rewards will vary according to the age of the recipient. Throughout the other chapters, I've set down some rewards that other parents have told me have worked in their families.

## Personal Preferences
Ask everyone what they think they need in terms of materials. If your kids think that doors on closets are dumb (most do), take them off. Maybe they'd like crates instead of dresser drawers. One idea that's worked is to put a lot of shelves into closets and let the kids decide what to do with them. But don't get carried away with organizing tools such as crates, shelving, clear plastic boxes, and the like. A certain amount of them help, but they aren't the long-term solution. That's losing sight of the goal. The goal is to get rid of clutter, not store it neatly. If you don't have the right spaces for the stuff that the family needs, then, by all means, go to Clutter Depot. Remember, though, less is more.

## Have a Competition
The real goal is to get rid of stuff the family no longer needs, so keep a record of how many pounds of clutter each family member has gotten out— perhaps make it a competition. Because 40 stuffed bears won't weigh as much as the barbell set nobody uses anymore, give credit for volume, too. I've found that the "losing weight" trick is a great motivator.

"Mike, when you came to my house and suggested weighing our clutter as we got rid of it, I was skeptical. But you know what? That was the biggest motivator after you left. In a way, I felt like it was the weight I hadn't lost after my first child. The kids loved it and turned it into a competition."

—Sandra,
a cluttering mom

## Communication

When anyone doesn't do his share or clutters, don't pick up after him. Don't nag. He's aware of what he's doing. Talk about it. Find out what's really going on. This book is ostensibly about decluttering your family, but it's really about communication.

## Managing Time

Both adults and kids have crowded schedules, with athletic activities, music lessons, dance, karate, and the chauffeuring that goes along with all that, but emphasize that keeping the family's living space neat is an activity too. If there's not enough time for that, then something's wrong.

# Housework Is Not Decluttering in Itself

I know that in today's hectic world, just finding time to do the housework is tough enough. Now would be a good time to explain that housework and decluttering are two different things. You can use this to your advantage by differentiating the two. When you or your children get tired of decluttering, which is both cerebral and emotional, switching to housework, which is rather mindless, can be a good change of pace, yet keep you in a decluttering mood.

Here's how they differ: Housework involves very few decisions. There's not a lot of personal attachment to dirt (at least for most of us). While we may have great memories of a meal, that's never an excuse not to wash the dishes afterwards. Yes, picking up things from the floor and sofa seems to be both housework and decluttering, but there are really two separate processes going on. The picking up part is easy. That's housework. The putting away part is harder. That's decluttering. That requires some thought.

The good thing about switching from decluttering to housework is that it is a physical activity. Decluttering can be frustrating. Kids can take out the frustration they might feel at not being able to decide what to eliminate by pushing a broom, scrubbing a sink, or pushing a vacuum.

## What Is Hoarding?

Hoarding is filling areas with so much of little or no value that it is impossible to live or function in those areas. It is extremely distressful, sometimes to the point of being mentally debilitating. Clutterers are basically clean people. However, those with obsessive-compulsive disorder (OCD) who also suffer from compulsive hoarding are another story. They do live in filth as well as clutter. Fortunately, they are less than one percent of the population and almost never have children living at home. Children also may have OCD, but generally with other manifestations (hand washing, counting, excessive fear of germs, and so on). If your child begins to hoard, it is a definite sign that something more serious is going on. Hoarding can also be found independently of OCD, and may occur in conjunction with other mental and psychotic disorders, but is a serious condition in any case.

Hoarders could be expressing some emotional trauma that they can't deal with. It may be a sign of abuse, according to Kim Cooper, M.Ed., a family therapist and neurobehavioral psychometrist who has worked extensively with abused children. However, some mothers of kids with learning disabilities told me that their children tend to hoard too and there's no abuse in their families. So don't jump to conclusions about the cause. Try to find out what's going on by communicating or, if necessary, with professional counseling, but don't just ignore it.

Clutterers sweep the floors where they can and, if they are lucky, can vacuum the paths between the boxes and piles of papers that litter their floors. If your house fits this description, the later chapter on cluttered spouses is for you. If, however, your house is relatively tidy, your carpets are to be walked on (not to be used as staging areas), and the only paths are in your garden, then you can teach your children housework easily.

# Kids Change

No one knows for sure if cluttering is genetic, but I lean toward it being either a learned behavior, a control issue, a reaction to life's stresses, or rebellion. If my childhood is any indication, I should have turned out to be a neat adult. I wanted to be a good little boy. I didn't become a card-carrying clutterer until much later. I helped wash the dishes at a very young age. Fortunately, breakage was minimal, or at least not enough to upset my mom.

There's a lesson here. When your child of any age actually helps with some of the housekeeping, accept that the job won't be done perfectly and that some breakage is part of the package. (To be practical, buy inexpensive dishes for everyday use.) Please don't react with anger or negativity. Do that now and you'll undo all the positive things that got you both to this point. Praise your child for what she does right. If she breaks something, either by sweeping too enthusiastically or dropping dishes when washing or drying, don't fly off the handle. Instead, let her know that's not quite the way it's supposed to work out, and let her get out the broom and dustpan to clear up the wreckage.

## Life Lessons From Cleaning

I became a dish-washing fool and even washed dishes for an elderly blind lady down the road from my childhood home. It made me feel good to help her. I learned that doing for others was a good thing and that I had a skill I could use to help others.

An interesting outcome of my helping the elderly lady was that I learned a couple of valuable lessons. First, she was African-American and I am Caucasian. I didn't know what that meant, only that she was a nice lady and I liked being around her. Later, other kids asked me why I was hanging around with her and used the "N" word. I had to ask my mom what it meant and got a good lesson in not growing up with prejudice.

Secondly, she named me in her will, to the consternation of her family, who didn't come to visit her. My parents wouldn't take the property she left me, but made me appreciate how doing little things for others can mean a lot to them. The reward was how I felt, not the material things. It also taught me not to judge people by outside appearances. To most people, she lived in a shack. It turned out that she owned a big chunk of the town of Las Cruces, New Mexico. Those were some pretty powerful life lessons gleaned from liking to wash dishes!

# Anger

There are a few absolutes that definitely do not work for anyone (such as nagging, belittling, saying *"You'll do it because I say you'll do it,"* humiliating, and hitting). It's hard not to get angry with your kids when you trip over their toys on the stairs or their bikes on the walk when you're late for work. We're going to eliminate the source. If you have to get angry, get angry with the clutter, not the kid.

Cluttering may be your child's way of expressing anger. Kim Cooper, M.Ed., a family and anger management counselor and neurobehavioral psychometrist with the University of Texas Medical Branch, with 10 years experience working with adults and children, told me, "Kids are scared to be angry with adults. They need to be taught that the only time anger is wrong is when we act on it."

An interesting note on decluttering techniques is that, although not very spiritually aware, for some people anger is a great motivator to decluttering. It works for me. I find that when enough stuff builds up and starts stealing my space, I get angry with it and can deal with it. Whatever works, works.

## Accept That There Will Be Mistakes and Don't Yell at Your Kids

By the time I got to third grade, I got into ironing. Part of it was a little boy fascination with using a tool, and part of it was pride in my appearance. Because my parents had owned a motel, we had a commercial ironing machine. Yes, I did scorch a few shirts, and, yes, I learned that, with starch, less is more, but I never got yelled at for it.

My dad was an avid gardener before he graduated to being a farmer. Early on, I liked digging in the earth (what little boy doesn't like getting dirty?) alongside him. Very few of the seeds I planted sprouted, but the ones that did made me feel pretty good about myself. And my dad, for all his faults, didn't get upset with me for not doing it right. I know now that it took tremendous effort on his part, and I am grateful.

If your child makes a mistake, and you feel that you need to discipline him, consider the crime first. Discipline works better than punishment, though it's harder on the parent, because it requires some thinking. I was disciplined a lot as a child (okay, maybe I wasn't that good), but I don't remember specific incidents. I do remember the times I was punished. I was once punished, at about age 5, for imitating my dad's sign-painting by adding a few splashes of color to a billboard he'd painted. In a way, the one punishment was successful—I never touched my Dad's paints again. But I never wanted to paint again either.

Lest you start to worry that learning to not-clutter will stifle the creativity of your child, there's a chapter about that issue. But first, let's get to the practical stuff.

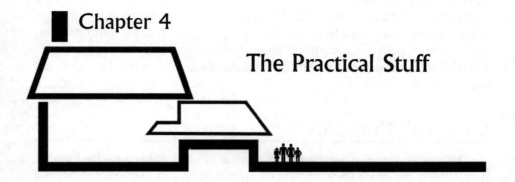

# Chapter 4

# The Practical Stuff

*I got tired of having to pick up after my kids. I started to pick things up, but put them in a special closet. To get back their dolls, toys, or shoes, they had to pay a ransom. A quarter a shoe seemed reasonable. In a way, I was sad when the lesson took hold. I missed those extra quarters.*

—Dan, a good parent of three beautiful children who made it to adolescence

*My kids appreciate a sense of space. They like it better when everything is cleared. As soon as they have a big open space to run around, they seem happier. When they mess up an area, they move to another open area."*

—Trudy, mother of six

Cluttering kids are inventive. They'll find new ways to clutter, so you'll need different tools you can adapt to outwit, I mean teach, them. What works with one child may not work with a sibling. Gee, I'm sorry to make you work, but I've given you choices rather than a set of rules.

Kids are individuals, just like you. What worked with your 3-year-old won't work with your 8-year-old or your teenager. But something always works. There is always hope.

Even though all of my books on living a clutter-free life have chapters on practical applications of my decluttering principles, I'll never forget the reviewer who lambasted my book *Stop Clutter From Stealing Your Life* by saying that it was great for hand-holding but shy on how to clean up your messy room. I was quite hurt by the review, but now I thank that reviewer, because he taught me something about communicating with my audience. The tips were there, but towards the middle of the book, after I'd explained the "why" of cluttering.

## Okay, Call Them Tips

This time, I'm putting the "tips" section in earlier, because that's what people look for when they buy a book in this genre. But you've got to read the whole book. These aren't all the tips. They pop up throughout the book, after the "whys" are explained. My books aren't just about tips; they're about changing your life.

You want tips you can use right now to solve specific problems. There are a lot of them here, but please don't stop without reading the "why" as well as the "how-to" parts of this book. Tips on how to organize are certainly necessary. We all can use a refresher on the "how-to" part of decluttering. But my basic philosophy is that without understanding the "why" of cluttering, the tips are short-term measures. Tips are commonsense things you already know, for the most part. But by incorporating a number of them into one chapter, you'll probably see some that you'd never thought of before.

## Cluttering Reasons and Solutions Aren't Age-Specific

Decluttering and not-cluttering principles are pretty universal no matter the age of your children, with a few modifications. Teens deserve a chapter all their own because there's a lot more going on with them and some different ways of reaching them. The main difference in age groups is that the older they get, the more different kinds of stuff they accumulate.

That said, I recently consulted with a cluttering family whose 2-month-old baby already had so many clothes and toys that she had a drawer for each month she was old, two cribs, enough stuffed animals to start a snuggling zoo, and books. She was well on her way to becoming a clutterer.

## Communication Is the Key

The real key to implementing systems is communication. Cluttering is about control. If you involve your kids in the designing of systems for your house, you give them a sense of control over their possessions and their lives. You and your children will probably come up with new ideas that will work for your family. Sometimes something will work for awhile and then no longer work. Rather than being rigid and "beating a dead horse," work with your children on trying something else that will work.

Every child is an individual. They aren't robots or extensions of yourself. There's no one "right way" to organize that'll work for all kids all the time, any more than there's one right way for all adults. There are some practical things you can do to encourage not-cluttering behavior and help build habits of picking up.

You can implement all the systems in the world, but if your children clutter because of psychological issues, you and they are going to have to deal with them before systems will have lasting effects. And there will be times when the systems break down. I've tried to give some general principles that should apply in most cases, but not be too rigid.

## Make It Easy

- Make it easy to put things up.

- Brightly-colored boxes are better than dull cardboard ones.

- Put shelves and drawers at kid height instead of adult height. To figure out how high that is, watch your children as they try to put things away. Let their actions speak louder than anyone's words.

- If they seem to balk at putting certain items up, either the item is too big or too heavy and should go on the floor against the wall, or the designated space is too high.

- Because this is a lifelong learning experience, adjust the height of the homes for stuff as your kids grow older, if it seems like they're having a harder time putting their stuff away.

    Some organizers suggest making things harder to get out than to put away. I don't. To me, that encourages a belief that decluttering has negative consequences. The reason for decluttering should be the pride of having a neat room—a positive habit that's just part of life.

- Say good-bye to that ornate toy box. Clear plastic containers are best for just about everything. If kids can see their stuff, they like it better. Plus, they won't have to unpack everything in a box to find that special toy, game, or doll they just have to have right now. We all know that when stuff escapes its box, it has a hard time being corralled back into confinement.

- Help your children learn the wonderful world of grouping by type. Dolls are one type of item that lives together. Toy dishes go together, as do toy tools. Building pieces and other odd-shaped or non-stackable items live in a bucket, like crabs. Things that can be stacked like sardines go into flat containers.

# Apply Learning Modalities

## Visual Learners
Especially if your children are visual learners, use see-through plastic crates so they won't feel like putting things away is losing them. Wire shelves help these children. Anything that hides items bothers them.

## Logical Learners
If they're logical learners, emphasize that like things go with like things. These kids will pick up on the concept that it's more efficient to put things back, so they won't waste time trying to find them later.

## Auditory Learners
For kids with a strong auditory sense, encourage them to say "until later," "hasta la vista," "goodnight," "buenas noches," "buena serra," "gut nacht" (heck, why not teach them a little foreign language to make it more interesting?) or something to their toys and games as they put them in their assigned homes. This helps them create a mental hook to the location of the items and eases their fears of not being able to find them again.

## Kinesthetic Learners
If they're kinesthetic learners, just the act of picking things up, carrying them to their homes and putting them away may be enough for them. If not, encourage them to pat the item as they put it up. This could be an obsessive behavior, if they have to pat it a certain number of times or perform some

other sort of ritual, so keep your eyes open. Don't freak out if they do pat stuff a few times. You're not going to give your kids OCD, but if they already have a proclivity in that direction, this could be an indication. It'll only be a warning sign if they pat things three, five, or some specific number of times, every time. A few love pats are normal.

### A Picture Is Worth a Thousand Explanations

Labels take decision-making (the hardest part of decluttering) out of putting things away. Pictures work best for younger children. Named labels of what goes where works for older children—until they're old enough to think it's dumb. But by then, they may think you're dumb too, so what's the difference? Cut out a picture of each item or group of items that lives together, from magazines or the boxes things came in, and tape it to the shelf or drawer where it's to be put. Socks, underwear, and T-shirts generally cohabit the same space (and multiply exponentially). You could put pictures of the three items, or a model appropriately dressed.

- Books all go together, so one picture of a book will make it easy to remember where to put them.

- Games are all different, but board games live on one shelf, so a picture of one of them should suffice. Plus, it'll help your children learn to associate items by type.

- Large items such as robots and video game systems with cartridges take up a lot of room but should have a shelf or certain amount of floor space allotted to them. Put up a picture of each one, or something that represents "big toys."

- Come to think of it, that's probably a good idea for the garage for all of your partner's big toys (power tools, gardening tools, and so on) that never get put up. (Some adults might benefit from the same pictures of clothing taped to the dresser. On the closet door, put a picture of a laundry basket with a big red X across it).

## Make It Interesting and Educational

Decluttering is inherently boring, so add a little interest to the process:

- In addition to the pictures, add labels with the name of each item or group of items in a foreign language.

- Who knows, this might pay off in a child who develops a love for linguistics. Try several of the major languages: Spanish, French, German, Italian, or even Russian or Chinese. This is especially useful if a language other than English is spoken in your house.

- Change the language once a month or so. This will give your children something to look forward to and make the putting-away or decluttering process more interesting.

# If Something Comes in, Something Goes Out

One way to stem the flow of more stuff into your children's lives is to establish a couple of rules. If they "need" something new, they "need" to eliminate an item from their hoard of possessions. Everything has a cost associated with it beyond the purchase price. Every single item we bring into our lives takes a certain amount of free space from us. Solid objects displace space. Each item requires some sort of maintenance, even if it's only finding a place for it, moving it from time to time, and cleaning it. We have a finite amount of space; we can't fill it with an infinite number of items.

If you doubt that every thing has a price beyond what it costs, consider this quote from the American Red Cross Website (*www.redcross.org/donate/goods/*) about why they don't want donations of things: "Collections of items require valuable and scarce resources such as time, money, and personnel to sort, clean, and distribute them...."

## Decluttering by Proxy

You may have one child who enjoys putting things away and another who hates it. Often, the non-enjoyer will pay the enjoyer to put up his things. If your cluttering child becomes magically neat, he may have been visited by the decluttering angel and miraculously transformed into a neat person. But before you run to your priest, rabbi, or minister with a tale of divine intervention, keep an eye on him. It's more likely that he's bribing a sibling to pick up after him.

Don't accuse. If he's really learned to not-clutter, you'll destroy his sense of accomplishment and you'll be in a worse place than when you started, because he'll feel penalized for doing "right."

Praise him for the good job and ask him what changed. If he averts his eyes (an involuntary reaction to lying or thinking up a good answer), suspect the worst. Watch closely when it's time to pick up his toys or room.

While children are pretty smart, it's still hard for them to outwit most adults, most of the time. You may have raised a budding CEO who knows how to delegate, but this isn't the time to learn that skill. Should you catch the little darling delegating, explain again why it's important to clean up his own messes. A little discipline wouldn't be out of line. The enabler who helped isn't at fault. He was only learning how to be an entrepreneur.

## Family (Common) Areas

If there's one area that needs to be decluttered on a regular basis, it's the area shared by all of the family. If you have adult clutterers in the family, they'll have to pitch in too. Because this is a bit more complicated than the other parts of the house, tips on that are included Chapter 3 and other parts of the book.

It'll be hard to teach your kids to not-clutter or declutter the common areas until the other cluttering members get involved. It's very unmotivating to pick up your own clutter when there's so much of someone else's that you can't see a difference.

Hold a family meeting, because this is a family problem. Explain that the family rooms are for everyone and, if any one person clutters, it hurts the whole family. Ask for your kids' help. Explain that you have a tough enough time taking care of the house and that their involvement would make your life easier.

## Make It a Game

First, try to make it a game for the kids to declutter the family room. Whoever picks up all of his stuff in the least amount of time wins. Make some appreciable reward for winning. Have a second (and equally valuable) reward for the most stuff picked up. The child who's cluttered the most won't be able to win the first reward, so make sure she has some motivation too. If that doesn't work, try a little logic, then a penalty.

## Use Logic, Mr. Spock

Tell your kids in a calm manner that a pair of shoes left under the coffee table doesn't seem like a big deal, but it is. The same is true for dirty socks (ugh), toys, games, magazines, and books. You're tired of picking them up and putting them away, so from now on, you're just going to do the first part.

Warn them that if you have to pick anything up, it belongs in jail. You're the warden. Give them a week to get with the program. If that doesn't work, take Dan's suggestion, from the beginning of the chapter, about holding toys and errant shoes for ransom. Dirty socks, well that's up to you. Take the money out of their allowances or any money they earn. Things like losing the remote for the TV or the portable phone can result in losing the privileges associated with the item.

# Kids' Rooms

The most important decluttering tip is that your children should help decide where things go as soon as they're old enough to have ideas of what they want. Because cluttering is about controlling our space, give them the opportunity to determine how their space is going to be utilized. Think about it. If your boss autocratically implements a system at work, are you as likely to follow it than if you had some input?

## Closets

Little ones can hardly be expected to hang up their clothes. Neither can older children, if the closet hanging rod is higher than they are tall. Why make it hard for them? Put in wire shelves that serve double-duty. They can hang clothes from them and stack stuff on top. Consider eliminating the closet door entirely. Most kids just think a closet is dumb. Depending on how your children feel about it, you can put up a drape, or leave it open to give a sense of more space. For teens, a closet without a door or drape makes their room feel like an efficiency apartment. That gives them a sense of being an adult.

## Chest of Drawers

Some kids rank these on the scale of dumb adult ideas just below closets. Try crates. Heck, anything that makes it easier to put stuff away works.

## Clothing

If your kid "has" to have a new outfit, dress, or shoes, then she needs to make room for it. Sure, it seems like she can cram an unlimited number of dresses into her closet (sound familiar?), but it violates some law of physics. A closet crammed full of clothes means that some are seldom, if ever, seen again. I've heard parents swear that, in the dark of the night, their children's clothes breed and make more clothes. I believe it.

This concept should be applied before you go to the store. When he first says he needs new clothes, games, shoes, and so on, even before you get into the discussion about whether he needs it, if you can afford it or if it's appropriate, let him know that the rule is that he has to decide what to get rid of first. Ideally, "getting rid of" should mean passing it on to someone who can use it, not throwing it in the trash.

## Make an Inventory

Offer guidance, but don't make the decision of what to eliminate. Give them a chance to change the biggest obstacle to not-cluttering. A major reason clutterers hang onto stuff is that they don't want to make decisions on the relative value of what they already own.

"But Mom, I need all my clothes. I might wear them someday."

"I tell you what," you might say. "Why don't you make an inventory of your clothes? Write down each item, the last time you wore it, and what special occasion you're saving it for?"

If you're lucky, that'll keep them busy until they've grown another three inches. Then, the decision's already made. If it doesn't fit, it doesn't belong. Oh, if it was that simple! Some of the clothing items, for boys and girls both, are kept because of the memories they trigger. That's also true for adults. A certain amount of "memory clothing" is perfectly normal. But when we have stuffed our closets with memories of the past, we leave no room for the present or the future.

Sometimes, just being aware of what we own can help us from buying something new—we probably already have it!

The sample on page 54 shows how an inventory might look.

## Beds

Nothing your children can do with less effort will make more difference than making the bed. Sure, it's dumb. You're only going to mess it up in a few hours anyway. When they pull that excuse on you, ask if it applies to dishes. Should you never wash dishes because you're just going to use them again in a few hours?

The point of a made bed is that it's a visual focus for the room. When it's messy, it's easier to let the rest of the room slide. Military precision in bed-making is best reserved for the military. As long as the sheets are relatively straight and the cover is pulled back, call it a success.

## Sample Inventory

| Item | Condition | Last Worn | Saving For | Makes Me Feel/ Reminds Me Of |
|---|---|---|---|---|
| Pink dress | Good/fits | Last week | Use all the time | Pretty |
| Sweatshirt from concert | Ratty, stained | Six months ago | Don't know | The time Tommy took me to the concert |
| Old sneakers | Worn out/ too small | Don't remember | Don't know | Nothing special |
| Shirt with snaps | Excellent/ too small | Once since I bought it | Next cowboy event I go to | Dumb/ cowboy stuff isn't cool |

## Toys and Games

Designate shelves or floor space for these items. Remember the label idea to make it easy. Eliminating decision-making in decluttering is half the battle. You can win this one easily. Your kids may even get into the spirit of "organizing" by grouping the same types of games and toys with each other. This is an integral part of cognitive learning, so encourage it.

If your kids have so many toys that they don't have room for them, gently encourage them to pick out the ones they use the least (if at all) and give them to kids who don't have much. I favor giving things to women's shelters, because gifts to them go directly to kids who don't have much and have a hard enough life to begin with. Direct donations to families you know who are struggling are perfect. Your church or civic groups may be able to give directly. Give where it counts. One thing that holds adult clutterers back is that they feel like they have to donate things to "just the right person or organization." This makes it easy.

## Clear Space

Don't forget to include some space between items. If your kids learn early on that "white space" is an important part of decorating, they'll be less likely to cram every shelf with stuff. Feng shui is a rather complicated concept, but one aspect that's easy to incorporate is that clear space is a valuable part of the whole.

## Stuffed Animals

"When I bring newly purchased items into my cluttered home, there is a good chance they could get lost or damaged. Sometimes I don't even get to use the object for the first time! This feeling of indifference and lack of respect for my own property is very familiar. I think it first showed up in my life after an experience I had when I was 7 years old. At that time I had a teddy bear that was very special to me and that I loved dearly. I came home from school only to discover that he had been completely ripped to shreds by the family dog! I scanned the room in disbelief. All that was left of him were numerous pieces of spit-soaked fur and fluff.

"I never replaced that bear with another special bear. Instead, I collected a random assortment of stuffed animals, none of which I was all that fond of. With an air of cool indifference, I treated them equally. Perhaps this attitude was a way of shielding myself from future pain. If I could harden my heart then maybe it wouldn't hurt so much the next time it got broken. The act of accumulating so many animals—an attempt on my part to fill the void created by the loss of my original stuffed animal—turned out to be a destructive habit. The animals got shuffled around, serving no purpose other than to add to the clutter of the room."

—Janie,
a clutterer

Dan's daughter has 120 stuffed animals. This menagerie is cataloged. Way to go, Chelsea! A few stuffed animals are going to live on the bed even into the teenage years. Encourage your children to find a balance between the comfort of these animals and the danger of being suffocated by them.

If your kids have so many stuffed animals that they'll never be able to play with them, encourage them to donate them to women's shelters and the like so that other kids who aren't as fortunate can have some. The sooner they learn to give, the sooner they'll learn to break the cluttering cycle.

## Clothes and Shoes

Here's a great opportunity to learn how to not-clutter. Help your children go through their clothes and shoes and pick out the ones that have stains or need mending. If you're handy at mending, you can do that for them—if you really want to. If, however, that's not your forte (or if you are a clutterer with so many "to be mended" items in your sewing room that you could start your own resale shop), help them understand that others can benefit from them more than they. A closet or chest of drawers so stuffed with clothes that they all get wrinkled just causes double-duty. The good ones have to get ironed (ugh) and the not-worn ones make it hard to decide what to wear.

Some clothes are going to be "memory clothes" and your children won't get rid of them no matter how bad they look. This is especially true when there's been a divorce or death. Don't press the issue. We all keep memory items. These are clothes or anything that reminds us of who gave them to us or where we went when we wore them. Eventually, you can teach your children that memories are best kept in the head, not the closet, but make this far down the list.

## Computer Clutter

Because it's a big part of modern life and a big source of clutter, Chapter 5 is entirely devoted to this subject.

## Study Space Rules

I'm not a big fan of the "R" word, but a couple won't permanently stunt your kids' emotional growth.

Rule one: Whether your children have computer desks or the kitchen table to do their work, they should treat their study space as backpackers treat the wilderness. When hikers come out of their trekking area, they try to leave it as if they'd never been there. Make it one of those dreaded "rules" that nothing goes on the desk but what's needed for the task at hand.

Rule two: The task isn't over until the desk is returned to its clear state. If your children learn this now, they'll have an easier time in an office, laboratory, or whatever environment they end up in to make a living.

Rule three: Stop studying 15 minutes before it's time to quit and neaten up. You can help them with this, because they probably have a poor sense of time. Announce halfway before it's time to clean up that study time will be over in "X" minutes. Books go back into the bookcase or backpack for school tomorrow. Papers are put into binders or folders or recycled. Glasses are taken back to the kitchen and washed or put in the dishwasher. CD's are put back into their jewel cases and refiled.

# Kitchens

Whether you're living in an efficiency apartment or a four-bedroom home, the kitchen is the easiest room to declutter. This is because, after the bathroom, it's the room least likely to be cluttered for emotional reasons, at least by kids. Parents may clutter it up because they can't throw away cottage cheese containers or butter tubs or some other sort of container. With clutterers, these items and cardboard boxes seem to hold a special fascination for us. If you're a clutterer, ask your children to deal with the incoming plastic containers. Unless you're ready, you probably won't want them to get rid of your stash of existing ones.

Because it's used every day, the kitchen is a good room to practice the habit of decluttering. From very early on, your children will probably want to offer a helping hand in the kitchen. With a little foresight, they could really help and not just make a bigger mess.

## The Reality of Food Preparation

I know that in today's world, big home-cooked meals aren't the norm. Many parents work outside the home. Even when there is a stay-at-home mom or dad, schedules don't always coincide. Kids require a lot of driving to and from scheduled events. Whether or not you agree that this is the way it should be, I'll leave to your own sense of values. From a practical sense, this is the reality.

Still, whether we eat take-out most of the time, or eat in the car on the way to something, there will still be some times when the family sits down to a real home-cooked meal. Today's dads are more likely to be the preparers than in days past. This sets a good example to offset stereotypes. Cooking and cleaning aren't just "women's work," as so many of us learned from our parents.

When children are very young, say up to age 5, they're unlikely to be much real help. But they can have their own set of dishes and toy cookware to "help" you as you prepare your meals. They may not be able to cut things yet, but they can surely be allowed to shred lettuce, take food out of bags, and other things that make them feel productive to the process.

## Make Their Space Their Height

A small table sized for them will work best for their needs. Having them stand on a chair to reach an adult-sized table is dangerous. Chairs topple and kids go boom. You may have to hand them things, which makes the process of preparing a meal less efficient, but there are more important things than efficiency.

## The Right Tools Make It Easier

Even small children can master an egg whisk. Heck, I can even handle one. Eggbeaters with a handle that turns require more dexterity. And the electric ones should be far down the list of tools to use. They've been known to get away from little hands, take off, and devour the family pet. Admittedly, the eggs may not be beaten into submission, but your kids will be so proud of having helped that it's best to overlook it at first. Later, you can help them improve their techniques.

As they get older, they'll be able to help even more. I was using knives at age 5, although I was a bit of a klutz, so it was probably dangerous. I know parents whose children of all different ages are allowed to help with the cutting-up process. It's probably best to give your children a small chore that involves cutting and see how well they do before you let them really get at it. A sharp knife is safer than a dull knife. Dull knives slip off the item being cut and invariably find a tiny finger, where they magically transform into scalpels.

One of my fondest childhood memories was learning how to sharpen knives at my father's side. I felt so grown up. To this day, whenever I sharpen a knife, I think kindly of him.

By the time your children are ready to help with the cooking, make sure you have oven mitts sized right for their little hands. A child who tries to grab a pot or take something out of the oven with an adult mitt is likely to drop it. Teach them to always use mitts, especially when taking something out of the microwave. I still have a hard time grasping that concept and get burned a lot. I mean, the bowls don't *look* that hot. Teach them that the plastic wrap is hiding mean old Mr. Steam, so mitt him.

While the height of the stove burners is fixed, you can get a step stool for your children. Again, a chair used for that purpose is a recipe for disaster.

## Kitchen Cleanup

Cleaning up is not the same as decluttering. Cleaning up is part of living. Decluttering is part of learning how to live less stressful lives. But when it comes to the kitchen, the two are more intertwined than anywhere else. The preparing, messing up, and consuming all happen together. When it's time to do the dishes, it's also time to put everything back in its home until you are ready to use it another day.

I believe that it's best to apply this lesson before the meal is ready. While things are cooking is a good time to wash (or put into the dishwasher) the utensils you used to make the meal. This is a more pleasurable time to do it than after everyone's eaten and there's a big mess to deal with. That's a chore. We're trying to make decluttering less of a chore and more of a natural part of the rhythm of life.

## Here's a Chance to Make Decluttering Pleasant

While the meal is cooking, the kitchen is filled with pleasant aromas. All the cooks are inwardly basking in a sense of triumph at having outwitted yet another pot roast or head of lettuce. It's also a good time to reinforce the understanding that decluttering is best done in small increments and that it is amazing what you can accomplish in 15 or 20 minutes.

## Adding Spice to Decluttering

Flour lives in a canister on the kitchen counter or the refrigerator, depending on what part of the country you live in. Spices live in the spice rack. Spice racks are great for teaching the joys of organization. Whether you've determined that they should be arranged alphabetically or by use, your children can catch the pride at putting them back where they belong. This will carry over to their own rooms, in the organization of their mementos, books, videos, and toys.

### Salads Teach Recycling Lessons to Aid in Other Decluttering

Debris from salad preparation either gets inherited by a gerbil, rabbit, or some other vegetarian member of the pet family, or goes to a compost bucket or the trash. This could be a lesson on how something can be recycled and on how, even though something is left, it may not be usable. This will make an impression for decluttering broken toys. ("Johnny, this toy is just like the half-used carrots we gave to the gerbil. You can't put it back together, but we can give it to someone who can. Goodwill [or your favorite charity] can fix it and pass it on to another lucky boy.")

## How to Get the Whole Family to Help Clean Up

A mother gave me this wonderful example of how the kitchen duties were performed in her home as a child. Her mom was having trouble getting the family to help clean up after dinner. Instead of yelling or ordering, she applied logic and strength:

"As long as this family is going to eat, there will be dirty dishes. If you wish to continue eating, you will all contribute to the preparing, cleaning, and maintenance of the kitchen. Now, I'm going to leave and you are all going to work out a schedule." With proud grace, she left the room and her speechless family to work out the details.

From that point forward, Dad and the kids did their part to make sure that their daily bread was put on the table, along with some meat and potatoes (or in today's world, pasta and soy products).

## Workshop Clutter

Boys and girls will probably express an interest in helping in the workshop. There's something about being able to fix and create things that inspires people. The suggestions for working in the kitchen apply here, just change the tools from eggbeaters to drills, knives to saws, and so on. Safety glasses are more likely to be used in the workshop than the kitchen unless you have a really creative cook.

Kids can carry small bits of lumber and hand nails and drill bits to their parent. They can sweep up. There's lots they can do without using the dangerous tools. As they grow older, they'll want to and should.

They can learn lots of decluttering lessons in a workshop. Everything has a home and has to go back there when you're done. They can get an idea of math from the different sizes of drill bits, nails, and from measuring wood to be sawed. Just like in the kitchen, their "help" will make things go slower, but so what? What's more important—that you get some project finished according to a time schedule or that your children bond with you and learn good habits? Hopefully, they won't bond to the various glues and cement you use.

As they grow older, you could let them design shelves and storage spaces for their rooms. That not only gets them involved in the process, it makes them appreciate the interconnectedness of things.

Not every kid is going to have a natural aptitude for shop working. I know it's hard to accept that your son or daughter just isn't as good as you at something you like, but stand back. If they don't like it, they don't like it. Not everyone is cut out to be a carpenter or a pianist. Everyone deserves the chance to find out, but shouldn't be forced to because it fulfills their parent's ideas of what they should be. Besides, if they choose not to help, you'll get your retreat back.

The following section about mechanics applies to this area of life too. Clutterers need to accept that they can't do all things well. I used to have dozens of tools, figuring I should be able to do handyman work. I even haunted garage sales scouting for more. All I achieved was an excuse to hang on to broken items because I was going to fix them someday and a few visits to the emergency room. A big part of learning not to clutter is to use our time wisely. Mine was better spent calling someone who knew what he was doing.

## Auto Mechanic Clutter

Learning mechanics from a parent can be a great experience. Or it can be the pits. If kids want to, encourage them. Take them to a first-class mechanic shop so they'll appreciate that everything has a place. Each mechanic takes care of his own stall. A cluttering tendency you can nip in the bud is to discard used parts when you replace them. Holding onto old spark plug wires, spark plugs, fuel pumps that don't pump, and so on, is a great temptation. Please don't succumb. When something's broken, it's trash. Let it go. Believe me, some spouse down the road will thank you for this lesson.

Again, not every kid is going to have skills at this. If they don't, you can teach another valuable not-cluttering lesson. Clutterers think they have to be able to do lots of things they can't do very well. That's why their houses and garages are filled with things that don't work. Learning what we're good at and accepting what we're not good at is an important part of self-acceptance. Teach it to them.

## If You Have Housekeeping Help

Just because you have someone who's paid to do the cleaning doesn't mean she's paid to declutter for your children. Frederica Kotin, a teacher and a parent, gave me this story:

"When I was a young girl, I would leave my clothes on the floor and books wherever I happened to stop reading them. My mother asked me to pick them up and I said, 'No. That's what the maid's for.'

"The next day Mother told me that all people deserve respect, no matter what they do for a living. The housekeeper's job was to clean, not to be my servant. She said, 'I'm going to do something that will help you to understand how hard it is to have to clean and pick up after someone else.'

"I was told to go to my grandmother's house every day for three months and pick up after her. She lived across town and I had to take busses to get to her. It was cold and rainy much of the time. I learned a lot about respect for people and things from that. This was an important lesson for any child. To this day, I respect people for who they are, not what they do. I also pick up after myself and taught my children to do the same. I wish more of my students had learned this lesson of respect. It is so often missing."

The goal of all of these tips is to promote respect for the things we have and the people who share our homes. Keep that in mind and they will be far more valuable than mere tips on how to keep your kids' stuff organized.

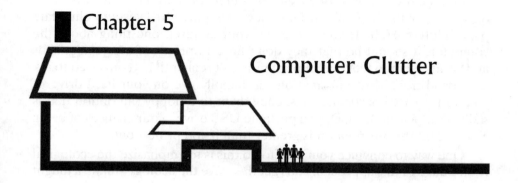

# Chapter 5

# Computer Clutter

*Mike, help! I bought my daughter her own computer, thinking it would help her in school. Now I don't know. Her room is awash in printouts of e-mails, Websites, and revisions of school projects and she can't ever seem to find anything. What's wrong?*

—Willie, a parent

I know a lot of adults' eyes will glass over when they see the title to this chapter. Don't worry. I've made it pretty basic, without using a lot of geek terms. Okay, "CD-ROM" and "USB" did sneak in, but your kids will know what they are. If, however, you still need your kids to read this to you, don't be ashamed. It could be their chance to read you a bedtime story. For the computer savvy among you adults, you can benefit from the information here too.

I've been working with, programming, building, and cluttering with computers since 1981. I love 'em. They're just one more example of how cluttering adapts to the changing times. Your kids are going to work with computers in some fashion, even if you don't have one in your home. They offer a great tool to overcome cluttering and disorganization, but are so often misused that they create more clutter and encourage a clutterer to save more stuff. One of the reasons people clutter is that they have a fear of not knowing something they should. Computers have a lot of information. You and your kids will never know it all. You don't have to.

# Printout Mania

Oh, the broken promise of the computer. Back in the early days, most of us fell for the hype about how they'd simplify our lives and eliminate paper clutter. Hah! If you can teach your children one thing about the computer, it should be that they don't have to print out everything. Kids and adults seem to feel that information isn't real until it's converted to ink on a dead tree. Most information can happily live on your hard drive. If you want to save particular files, copy them to a floppy (an option that is sadly disappearing), a CD, or a portable USB drive. Your chances of being able to find the information is greater than if you print it out.

One way to convince your kids to do this is to emphasize the ecological friendliness of this approach. Kids get the "save the ecology" mantra taught to them at school, if not at home. They take great pride in being able to recycle. Not printing computer files is going a step further. If you don't waste the resource to begin with, you don't have to recycle it.

Another tool is to help them make the leap that all digital information is the same. They're going to download media files to CDs, not print them. They can actually use research information better on their computer screens than on paper. If they're using it for a school report, they can cut and paste the pertinent information and kill only a few electrons instead of a forest. Some enlightened schools accept assignments on disk or CD.

If they feel they have to print out photos, there's not much you can do about that, except let them and then follow up in a few weeks and ask them where the photos are and how often they've referred to them. Do this often enough and they'll realize that there's no point to printing them except for momentary gratification, which turns into clutter.

## But I Gotta Print It Out

The only way to win this war is to take it skirmish by skirmish. Sometimes there are legitimate reasons for printing things out. Your children may want to show an e-mail or something they found on the Internet to a friend who doesn't have a computer. They'll print a map to a party (or maybe even a cultural event—stranger things have happened). Or maybe they want to share some information at school with everyone. Fine. But let's try to teach a little decision-making—the biggest obstacle to overcoming a cluttering mentality.

Ask your children why they need to print it. If they can come up with a legitimate reason (or an excuse that sounds pretty good), let them. Ask what they're going to do with it when they've finished the presentation or when the party's over. If they're on the right track, the word "recycle" will pop up. If they're clutterers, they'll want to keep it for sentimental reasons or because they "might need it again someday." Rather than clue them in to the truth that "someday" never comes, let them keep the printouts. Then, every few months, make it a game or family ritual that all the things saved for "someday" be gathered up. Announce that someday has arrived. Do this often enough and you'll make your point.

Most families have ink-jet printers today. Save yourself a bundle of money and teach your children to print in black and white unless absolutely necessary. Web pages and some e-mails are colorful—often for no apparent reason. Another trick is to save Web pages as text files, so that they don't print the banners and sidebars if they aren't needed.

## Ah, Sentiment!

What if there's really some sentimental attachment? What if it's the photo of a new boyfriend or girlfriend? There's nothing wrong with sentiment. But when the crush has turned to crash, gently suggest that it's time to get rid of the pictures. The important life lesson that your children learn from this is that hanging onto possessions or relationships that have outlived their purpose isn't necessary.

But don't be ruthless. How many adults have pictures of former loves and family members we don't have any real attachment to? Ask your children to decide on a limit for the number of keepsakes, say three per person. That's an arbitrary number, so talk to your children and agree on a number that makes sense to both of you. This is another decluttering principle you're teaching. Clutterers hold onto things because they're afraid of forgetting the memories of the person attached to the physical item. If your children learn now that things don't equal people and it's okay to let the physical reminders go, they're more likely to trust their memories later. Gosh darn—you're teaching them to trust and use their memories. See, decluttering is about more than getting rid of stuff.

# Music CDs

With the advent of legal music file download sites, kids today are likely to download mixes of their favorite songs as well as buy entire CDs in stores, though store-bought CDs are still the biggest share of the market. Keeping them together and findable is your kids' clutter challenge.

Music CDs and DVDs create almost as much clutter as excess printouts. It's not unusual for kids to have hundreds of music, program, and data CDs. Apple's iTunes, RealOne.net, and MP3 Grand Cental already offer legal music downloads for $.79 to $.99. According to the International Herald Tribune Website (*http://www.iht.com/articles/118033.html*), "Microsoft,...Wal-Mart Stores, RealNetworks, Roxio, and MusicMatch sell or plan to sell music for downloading over the Internet. The market for legally downloaded music will be $35 million in 2003, said David Card, an analyst at Jupiter Research. He estimated that online music sales would rise to more than $100 million next year and approach $700 million by 2008."

The CDs and DVDs from stores have the title and artist visible on the jewel case. Downloaded ones need to have the same scheme. It will help if all CDs/DVDs are kept together, regardless of the source.

Invest in empty jewel cases (preferably the thin ones) and tiny labels for the edges. CDs, like anything else, are useless if they can't be found. If a kid's old enough to create a CD, he's old enough to make labels for it. Just like supper isn't over until the dishes are done and put away, downloading isn't done until the CD has been put in a jewel case with a label. You can invest in a program that makes labels or set up a template in your word processing program for your children to use. They're learning a valuable lesson on completion. Half-done projects are clutter. Make it easy to find treasures later and you'll hear fewer wails, "Mom, where's that CD?"

The CDs themselves should go into whatever storage scheme your child likes. What's important is that music CDs go together. Program CDs belong in their own rack. There are swivel CD racks, which I prefer, that are large enough to keep certain types of music (or programs) arranged by type. Because your kids' music CDs will mostly be one type (the kind you can't stand), they might arrange them by artist. Plastic trays or boxes for CDs are still available and they at least stack, but they're klunky looking. There are also wire rack towers that take up less space but leave a lot to be desired organization-wise. Kids, however, think they're cool. It's their stuff, so let them choose the style they like.

Letting your kids choose the storage solution that makes sense to them is a common not-cluttering theme. If you insist that they use something that makes it harder for them to relate to, they won't use it. Take them to the office supply or computer store and help them decide which ones they like. Don't go overboard buying containers for CDs or anything else. The goal is for them to set reasonable limits on how much stuff comes in and then get rid of items that are over the limit.

## Program CDs

Once you've installed a program, get rid of the box, please. Send it to recycling heaven. Program boxes take up a lot of room and serve no earthly purpose. Because many programs now come in paper sleeves with the serial numbers on them, they need to be put into the aforementioned jewel cases. Write serial numbers or installation codes on the CD itself with a felt marker and on a standard-sized label on the outside of the jewel case. Sometimes the two get separated, even in the best of homes. Besides, if you are reinstalling the program and the install key is on the CD, unless you're Superman, you can't read it inside the CD-ROM drive. Make sure that the version number is part of the information. Version 1 is not what you want when you need to restore a corrupted copy of version 5.

As I said before, programs live in an entirely different place than music or backup CDs. This teaches your children that, even though items may look similar, they aren't the same thing. This is an important skill for adult life. It may save your kids from later using the archaic method of filing papers (newest stuff is put on the top) or filing systems with folders named "Bills," "Interesting Stuff," or "Work I Don't Want to Do."

## Computer Desks

If you can't afford a computer desk for your kids, don't feel that you're depriving them. Many people, including me, worked on a variety of desks for years before "computer desks" came out.

The most important thing about a desk is that the keyboard is lower than the flat surface of the desk. That cuts down on carpal tunnel syndrome. However, even more important than that is an adjustable chair with arms. The chair arms support the kids' arms and that's crucial. If the chair is adjustable, it doesn't matter if there's a keyboard drawer or not.

I used to be a big fan of fancy computer desks. I rationalized that all the cubbyholes and drawers would help keep me organized. This is the "all I need is the right storage solutions and my clutter will be gone" theory. It's not dogma. It's heresy. Clutterers—children and adults—don't need more places to stuff things. They need to learn not to stuff their stuff. If you can afford to get your children a computer desk or two, do it. Fortunately, children's computer desks aren't as multifaceted as adult desks. Keep it basic.

I got rid of my clutterer's dream desk with four drawers, six cubbyholes, several shelves and God knows what else. Today I use a white drafting table with a slight downward tilt and a chair that adjusts to the height of the desk. I like the clarity of clear space. Maybe your kids will too. Ask them. It's easier to think in a clear space. As long as we are on the theory of a place to work, everything we put on our desk vies for our attention. It is no easier for your children to think at a cluttered desk than it is for you.

## A Little Filing Goes a Long Way

Even if your kids have learned not to print everything, they may still have a hard time finding information on their computers. This is because they haven't learned the basic principles of filing.

How to file things so we can find them again is a huge subject and took an entire chapter in *Clutter-Proof Your Business,* but here all we have to deal with is bits and bytes, not papers. It's simple, really. The skills your kids learn about filing on their computer will help them in the real world when they have to work in an office. Right now, it'll just relieve a lot of their frustration at not being able to find things.

### Computer File Organization Tips

- Don't dump everything into "My Documents."

- Make a hierarchical filing system. Any research, relevant Web pages, or papers they write go into specific folders under the subject. For example:

  **School stuff**

  History

  Geography

  Math

  Science

**Personal Stuff**

> Friends
>
> Dreams, Hope
>
> Cool stuff
>
> Diary

(And so on.)

They're learning to keep things that are their future separate from the present (school stuff). The more inventive will get more complicated than that, arranging subjects in school by date or by their current field of study, but this'll give them a head start.

# If You've Raised a Computer Whiz

At least you know he'll have a head start in finding a job, though that's still no guarantee as my unemployed IT professional friends remind me. But you won't have to cross that bridge for a long time. Meanwhile, if your child likes to tear computers apart and rebuild them, think of it as building a hot rod, in your day. Encourage him to join a user's group (oops that sounds bad, it's slang for a *computer* user's group). The advantage, clutter-wise, is that he'll be able to get rid of those spare parts he's replaced in his computer.

Computer people usually have at least one large box of hard drives that are too small, cables that may or may not work, and cards that probably have some use. They're really hard for us to get rid of. Just like auto parts clutter, they should be disposed of. You can't throw them into the trash either. Goodwill doesn't want old computers. Some technical schools will take them, but mostly they have to be recycled. If your kid's a member of a user's group, there's usually someone who thinks he can use the stuff. Of course, your kid may come home with new pieces of hardware, so apply the rule of "every new thing that comes in means an old thing goes out." Good luck.

## Even Computer Disks Get Cluttered

Encourage them to learn to defragment their hard disks on a regular basis. Teach them to back up important documents. When a computer crashes, it's too late. They can get a good lesson in what's valuable and what's not by periodically deleting files and programs they no longer use. If they can do it here, they'll be able to do it in the real world.

There you have it. See? That wasn't too hard to slog through, even for the non-computer literate (don't you just hate that term?), was it? If only all not-cluttering habits were as easy to learn as the ones from the computer, life would be simpler, wouldn't it?

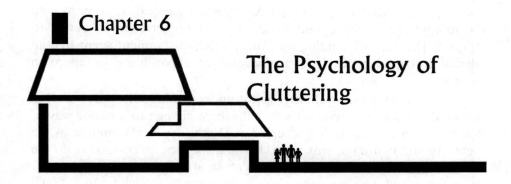

# Chapter 6

# The Psychology of Cluttering

*My belongings are a resource for the present and future, not a clinging to the past.*

—K.R.,
a clutterer

*With younger kids, you have to have more structure. With teens, they have to sign onto it. They sign on to these activities. They own them. Kids start something and stop it. And it is a mistake. Parents have to step back and use less control. Be more of a consultant.*

—Dr. Michael Bradley, Ed.D.,
author of *Yes, Your Parents Are Crazy*
and *Yes, Your Teen Is Crazy!*

Aw gee, this is one of those serious chapters. All you want is to have everyone pick up after themselves and to have some serenity in your house. The information here will help you understand what's going on in your family's cluttered minds, and you'll probably laugh at some of the examples. So read on and lighten up. You might want to jot down some psychiatry jokes in the margins if it gets too heavy.

Most of us know someone who is in, or we may have had our own personal experiences with, therapy. We see it as a last resort. Or we may equate seeking help from a psychiatrist as an admission of being crazy, weak, or lazy. After all, aren't we Americans supposed to be born with the ability to "get over it" and be able to "pull ourselves up by our boot-straps"? The idea of sending our kids to therapists might seem like an admission that we aren't doing a very good job of parenting—a failure on our part.

For us laypersons, psychology is just understanding the "why" of what people do and using techniques to help them change to a better way of doing it. You use psychology every day. Don't you, in the middle of the night, try and figure out why your children, spouses, or coworkers do the things they do? Congratulations! You're an armchair psychologist. Ever try to figure out why everyone else on the freeway is such a jerk? You'll probably never understand why, but you can apply psychology to yourself by knowing that your natural tendency to salute them with your middle finger will be counterproductive. That's psychology in action.

Later, we'll get into the serious issues of depression and anxiety, but right now, let's just try to understand some of the reasons why our children (and spouses) clutter. Understanding is the first step to changing behavior. Along the way, we'll learn some ways to communicate using simple psychological principles.

## Kids Do Things Because They Get Rewarded

It doesn't take a psychologist to understand that people do the things that give them rewards. What may be a little harder to understand is that people, especially kids, would rather get negative attention (a reward) than no attention at all. So, if you're reacting to your kids' cluttering, you're giving them attention. If you don't react to their not-cluttering, they aren't getting any payoff from it. They'll naturally do the thing that gets them noticed.

Psychologists say that the rewards for doing something, "reinforcers," cause people to maintain or increase behaviors. If a behavior is increasing or continuing to happen, it's being reinforced. Did you ever pull a prank on someone? If they didn't react, did you think, "where's the fun in that?" and stop doing it?

Reinforcing or rewarding "good" (acceptable) behavior works a lot better than punishing "bad" (unacceptable) behavior. So why is our tendency to focus on the bad rather than the good? Because it takes more work. Reacting to "bad" behavior is instinctive. Noticing "good" behavior and rewarding it requires higher thinking processes.

Johnny leaves his clothes on the floor. Kyla strews her schoolwork all over the dining-room table. We can't help but notice these events. We have an emotional reaction to them. We yell at them to "pick those things up."

### Action →Reaction →More Action

This feels effective because we are "taking action." We get rewarded on a primitive level by increased blood flow, which tells us that we are doing something.

Juan puts his clothes away. Sylvia picks up her schoolwork and neatly packs it in her backpack, ready to take to school the next morning. Unless we're there to watch them do these things, we don't know they've happened.

To effectively change behavior, your responses need to be consistent, reasonable, and immediate. In this case, the "immediate" part is when you notice it, not when it's done.

### Action →Nothing to React to → Thinking (What Is Different) →Realization →Reward

There are a lot more steps to noticing good behavior. One parent put it to me like this: "I expect my children to pick up after themselves. Why should I reward them for doing what they are supposed to do?"

Good question. If they can't get attention from the good things they do, they'll do what they know generates a reaction from you. Kids (and adults) do those things that get them noticed. Some kids and adults don't differentiate between positive notice and negative notice. They'll take whatever attention they can get. Pay attention to their positive behaviors and accentuate that. You'll be the one getting the rewards—kids who do what you want.

One of the reasons people clutter is that they can visibly see the results of their actions. Clear space isn't as obvious as cluttered space. We've been taught to revere stuff more than emptiness. Chaos conquers clarity.

## Control Issues

> "Although control sometimes provides the illusion of success on a short-term basis, children who are raised with both choices and responsibilities are more comfortable individuating under their parents' noses instead of going underground."
>
> —Jane Nelson, Ed.D., and
> Lynn Lott, M.A., from
> *Positive Discipline for Teenagers*

Cluttering is often about control. There are two sides to this. Parents may try to control their kids by dictating what's acceptable and what's not in terms of neatness. Children who chafe at that control may use their cluttering as a way of fighting back. In this scenario, both sides are fighting over control, not neatness.

Children feel they have very little control over their lives. Toddlers have the least; teenagers, the most. But even with teens, most of their lives are directed and controlled by others. It's common for parents to use an analogy that a child's job is to go to school, just like an adult's job is to go to the workplace. While this may work with smaller children, teens and precocious preteens will question this.

Adults have some control over their choice of work. Children have none whatsoever. They go to the schools their parents choose, are taught what the administration decrees, and are rewarded according to a set of values they had no say in creating. The only control they have is whether to do the work or not. Doing it returns a positive reward, though the value of the reward may not be sufficient to motivate them. Not doing it returns a negative reward, which may seem more rewarding to them.

So it can be with their possessions. Regardless of what techniques you use to motivate your children, they need to feel that they have control over the "things" in their lives. Whether they choose to exercise that control in a negative or positive way is dependent, to a large extent, on how you, as a parent, motivate them.

## Defining Control

It's a conundrum. If an adult or child chooses to clutter as an expression of controlling his environment, he apparently achieves control, but in fact, loses it. When we let our stuff define us, we give power (control) to the stuff. If your children choose to keep their rooms messy, the mess determines a large part of their interaction with the family and robs them of true freedom. A person's physical environment affects them, whether they're aware of it or not.

Clutter creates confusion and chaos on an emotional level. It fogs the mind, making it harder to do schoolwork or make decisions. Clutter's promise of control is an empty one. The clutter controls the reactions of their parents. If parents spend more time grousing about their children's messy room than complimenting them for a neat one, they're encouraging messiness. Negative attention is better than no attention.

When they leave their messes in the family areas, children, in effect, control the whole family. They see the reaction of family members and gain a sense of power from having determined the condition of the house.

The same is true for adults. When the cluttered spouse maintains the clutter, she maintains control. Families walk around the clutter. They've learned that picking up after an adult leads to confrontations or emotional outbursts. For the sake of peace, they've forgone harmony.

# Communication Is the Key
# to Changing Perceptions of Control

Do you feel like you spend way too much time complaining and nagging (Wait, you never nag, you only make suggestions. Sorry.) your children or spouse to "do something about this mess"? How well has that worked so far?

> "The biggest problem with any behavior disorder is a parent's fear of addressing the underlying causes. There's a fear of inadequacy, fear that emotions are wrong. They have to get over the designations of right and wrong when it comes to emotions. Emotions aren't wrong. They just are."
>
> —Kim Arrington Cooper, M.Ed.,
> family counselor and
> neurobehavioral psychometrist,
> UTMB

## Accentuate the Positive

My mother always saw the positive side of events. My father always saw the negative. She was happier and lived longer. Psychologist Dr. Richard Wiseman, author of *The Luck Factor*, said that people who look on the bright side tend to be luckier, have more friends, and be happier. By focusing on the positive, we have more positive experiences. Who knows? Maybe looking for the good in your clutterer's efforts will help you the next time you go to Vegas (though, to be honest, Dr. Wiseman says that is another form of luck, but I believe that a positive attitude helps there, too).

When your children or spouse actually pick up, recycle, or throw away something, congratulate them. If they've slipped into the negative mindset of cluttering, any improvement is a big hurdle for them to leap. We don't just wake up one morning and decide to change a lifetime of habits. We change slowly, replacing old beliefs with new ones.

The Texas two-step is a fun country-western dance. The *compliment* two-step goes nowhere. "Boy, that's great, Johnnie. You picked your schoolwork up off the dining-room table!" (a forward step). "BUT" (whenever we place "but" as the first word in a sentence, we negate the entire previous sentiment) "why didn't you get those books off the end table?" (a backwards step). Instead, learn to stop with the first step. Clutterers will eventually learn to declutter for the inner (intrinsic) rewards that being neater gives them. At first, though, extrinsic rewards from family members will have much greater value. If they get negative praise, they'll feed into the negativity, thinking, "Even when I make an effort, it's not appreciated. I might as well not have tried. Nobody appreciates how hard that was."

If your spouse is the clutterer in question, I know it's hard to get excited about a tiny bit of progress. Your whole house probably looks like you just moved in or are moving out. (If you've got a hoarder in the family, your house will look like you should be evicted.) One stack of papers moved, a few newspapers recycled, or a book put away doesn't make a visible difference. When you're in the mindset of seeing only the mess, you can understand what a clutterer's life is like. We see the big picture—the whole house or room. We feel like we can't declutter the whole house; it's just too overwhelming. What we eventually learn is to see the individual piles of clutter and to narrow our focus.

## Communicate Using "I"

Orders work just fine in the military. Families are more like the United Nations. I understand that sometimes gentle persuasion doesn't get the job done. Then you have to be a top sergeant—I mean parent—and tell your kids what to do. And sometimes you'll just get frustrated and yell at your kids. I don't know a parent who hasn't. Sometimes, as we say in the South, you gotta get the mule's attention to get him to move. But first, try the easier, softer way—communication.

Psychologists often have different ideas about how to approach things. Yet this is one area where most agree. When you make a statement using "You" or "Your (action)," you seldom get the results you want. "You" did this or that implies blame. Nobody wants to be blamed. Most people, including children, want to help. When your child is in a rebellious stage, you can throw that sentence out the window, but we'll have ways to cope with that later. Meanwhile, we'll assume that your children aren't perfecting their James Dean impressions yet.

I used to get bothered by sample conversations in books, because either I have a hard time learning dialogue or the people I'm talking to don't follow the script. Now I realize that they are put in books like these as examples, not scripts. Whatever you say, the key points are to use "I" statements instead of "you" or "you should" statements and to get your children to talk about how they feel about their clutter.

> "Not only were all our conversations turning into arguments, I was also telling my children over and over again not to trust their own perceptions, but to rely on mine instead."
>
> —Adele Faber and Elaine Mazlish,
> from *How to Talk So Kids Will Listen &*
> *Listen So Kids Will Talk*

Instead of: "You're a slob. Why can't you clean this room up?"

Try:      "I understand that your room is an expression of who you are. It's part of your individuality. But don't you think this room has created a new standard for messiness?"

If you get a "nah" or some other form of negative grunt, try another approach: "This messy room bothers me. What can we do to make it neater?"

Dr. Michael Bradley, in an interview, put it like this: "Have the kids separate the rebellion aspect. You might have the Starbucks conversation [at a neutral place away from the home]. 'I know your blood runs cold when I talk about your room. But does this hurt you by making you feel anxious in the morning or at night?' Give the kid observations and direction. 'Do you feel happy like that?'"

At one Clutterless Recovery Group meeting, one member was diagnosed with OCD. She brought a great insight to the group. "When my father complains about the way I act, I ask him, 'Do you think I like living like this?'"

In the beginning, before you've reached the point of making an action plan, vagueness is acceptable. Pretend you're a jungle hunter sneaking up on a wild beast at a watering hole. You proceed slowly, because the prey is wary and will bolt if it gets scent of a perceived enemy.

Instead of: "You never pick things up around the house."

Try:      "I get so frustrated and discouraged when I come home from work and the place is a mess. Can you help me? What can we do to fix that?"

You've taken the onus away from your children and placed it on you. You're the one who's frustrated. You've taken the personalities out of what frustrates you. The mess or the stuff frustrates you, not your children.

You never know, your kids might come up with the obvious suggestion that they pick up after themselves. At least give them a chance. But that's a vague concept. To make it work, you've got to get specific. You've laid some groundwork here to gain their cooperation. You've taken the very boring job of decluttering to the level of doing something nice for Mom and Dad. They don't understand a lot of the things they have to do to keep Mom and Dad happy, so this just gets lumped into the category of other inexplicable adult preferences. To them we are the ones from a different planet.

## Keep Your Suggestions Short and Explicit

In the last example, we talked about a big room or several rooms in the family area. Kids see the whole area and don't know what to do. The same is true for adults. Walk around the room that's bothering you with them and point out specific items that are their clutter. If your house is cluttered with other family members' stuff, your kids might point that out. Respond with something such as, "You're right, there is a lot of clutter here. Right now, we're working together on yours. Later, we can work with everyone else's."

"Is that your shoe?" "Are those your books?" "Are those your toys?" Getting your children to "own" their possessions is the first step. They can hardly deny it, unless they're really creative.

Follow up with a lesson you've probably already taught. *"Where do the shoes/toys/books live?"* This is still the information-gathering aspect of decluttering and although your children have most likely figured out what's coming next, they aren't threatened with having to do something yet. Any salesman will tell you it's important to get a potential client to get into the habit of agreeing before popping the purchase question. That's why they ask you so many personal questions and feed you questions that can be answered with a "yes" before telling you what their product costs. Consider this technique "parenting as a salesman." Sell the sizzle, not the steak.

Now, move in for the close. "You know, kids, it wouldn't take you much time to put the shoes/toys/books back in their home when you're finished with them, would it?" Follow up with another "yes" statement/question. "It would make me so happy if you'd just do that. Will you do that for me?"

"I guess so," may be the closest thing you'll get to a commitment, but it'll do.

Some parents follow up with a written contract, something such as, "I agree to pick up my toys and other things from the family rooms when I'm finished with them—every time." Their theory is that this formalizes the commitment. When people put something into writing, it reinforces the commitment.

Don't get too carried away with contracts or believe that a perfectly crafted contract will solve your problems. Dr. Bradley has a story in his book about a parent who thought he could solve all his rebellious teen's problems if he could just write a good enough contract for behavior that the kid couldn't find a loophole in. On the bright side, he may have raised a crackerjack lawyer.

### Apply This Same Concept to Their Rooms

You already know that children have shorter attention spans than most adults, except perhaps your boss. Vague directions such as "Clean up your room," are too broad.

Look at your children's rooms as if there was a laser beam security system like the ones at museums. The entire room is intersected with beams of lasers projecting a grid. Within each square of the grid is a foot or so of clear space. Within each foot of your children's rooms is a square foot of clutter. Work on one foot at a time. "Juanita, this whole room is just too much to do at once. Let's pick one very small area and see how well you can do with that."

Don't worry, your children won't graduate from college before they get one room done. As they get positive strokes for little things, they'll want to do more to get more strokes, thus making it easier on you and perhaps preventing you from having a stroke from opening their doors one day and being crushed by a mountain of clutter.

# Anxiety and Depression

"When I feel full of energy, I like to be in a clean room.
When I'm down, or feeling lazy, I like a messy room better."

—Megan, a preteen

It's normal for kids (as well as adults) to feel anxious at times. It's normal to feel "down" when things don't go right. Serious, persistent depression or anxiety needs to be treated by a psychological professional. According to Maurice Blackman, M.B., Fellow of the Royal College of Physicians of Canada (FRCPC), "Recent studies have shown that greater than 20% of adolescents in the general population have emotional problems and one-third of adolescents attending psychiatric clinics suffer from depression" (from *www.mentalhealth.com*, which is an excellent site for professionally written and researched mental health information of all kinds).

It would be out of the scope of this book to get into a full-blown discussion of depression and anxiety, but it is necessary to make a point about the relationship between those conditions and cluttering. When a kid (or adult) is depressed, he's more likely to clutter. In fact, if your normally neat child starts to retreat to his room and the room starts to get more and more cluttered, it could be a warning sign of a depressive episode. If the kid has always had a challenge with cluttering, decluttering will help his mood. When a kid clutters, her environment contributes to depressed feelings. It's hard to be upbeat when you're surrounded by a mess. Clutter saps children's energy, just as it does adult's energy.

Does cluttering cause depression? Nah. The causes of depression are way more complicated than that. Does depression cause cluttering? It certainly doesn't help. Depressed individuals lose interest in their surroundings and get easily overwhelmed. Those feelings are common to the clutterers I've worked with. Decluttering requires a lot of decision-making, which can cause anxiety. By teaching your children why to stay uncluttered and to declutter their environment, you're helping them to create more positive environments for themselves and not add to their stress. Living uncluttered can help their mental health.

## Rebellion and Purple Rooms

Kids, especially teens, need to rebel in order to individuate, or define themselves. If they don't rebel now, they will later. By making compromises with your kids regarding their own private space, you enable them to express their rebellion in a safe, yet satisfying way. Don't compromise on the family areas in terms of picking up after themselves, but you can compromise on when chores get done. Does it matter if the garbage gets taken out at 5:00 in the afternoon or 10:00 at night? As long as he's doing what needs to be done, let him do it when he wants.

When I asked Dr. Bradley about the rebellion aspect, he suggested a way to allow a little controlled rebellion: "Make a deal. 'If you want to paint your room purple and green, I will buy the paint and help.' Kids don't believe in drawers. How about crates? Let him make it art deco. It becomes the kid's room, like a studio apartment."

If your kid wants wild and crazy carpet in the room, let him put it in. Wait, that's probably too broad a statement. Let him choose it. Speaking as someone who tried laying carpet, get someone who knows what he's doing to put it in. You can rip it out when he leaves for college. Meanwhile, he feels that he has made his statement and successfully rebelled against your old, fuddy-duddy standards. You both win.

I ran this by several kids, from junior high to high school age, and they unanimously agreed this was a good idea. One father who followed through with this idea said this:

> "I thought the decorating ideas my son had were dumb and we fought about it at first. Then it dawned on me that we were fighting about his wanting to be an adult and have control over his living space. He's a good kid, so why waste our energy and shut off communication over this? He is the one who has to live there.
>
> "We made a deal. He agreed to keep up his chores and to pick up his shoes, clothes, and whatever else he brought into the family area. He agreed that he would still maintain a neat room. Guess what? He did keep it neat and showed real pride in his room for the first time. He asked my advice on what kind of paints and brushes he needed. He didn't have a clue about how to put up shelves. We worked together to make his room the way he wanted it. It turned out the old man did know a thing or two. We talked while we worked together and I learned a lot about what was going on in his world. Our family stress level went down. He has his friends over more often. I'd rather they were here than meeting somewhere else. It wasn't such a dumb idea after all."

# AD/HD

Attention deficit hyperactivity disorder is so important in any discussion of cluttering that all of Chapter 8 is devoted to it.

# OCD (Obsessive-Compulsive Disorder)

Relax, your kids probably don't have this disorder, but it's still important to know about, because cluttering, in general, often takes on some aspects of being compulsive. When I first started writing about cluttering, most of the literature was about hoarding. What I've discovered since is that cluttering behavior has some OCD components, some AD/HD components, and a lot of anxiety and depression components. It's like a computer made with old and new technology: It works, but not very effectively. There will be conflicts from different sets of hardware preferences.

Obsessive-compulsive disorder usually begins in the teenage years or young adulthood, though some recent studies suggest that younger children develop this disorder and haven't been diagnosed. We're all familiar with stories of children who continually wash their hands or count or exhibit "checking" activities (repeatedly making sure doors are locked, for instance). Hoarding is the OCD manifestation that relates to cluttering (although, as discussed previously in Chapter 3, hoarding can manifest independently or in conjunction with other conditions). We are more likely to see that in older adults, but it does happen with kids. Fortunately, the incidence of OCD in the general population is about 2 1/2 percent, and hoarders are about a third of that, according to one of the most respected experts in the field, Dr. Gail Steketee.

If a kid has OCD tendencies, they are more likely to show up as being excessively neat than being excessively messy.

"Teenagers with OCD have obsessions and/or compulsions. An obsession refers to recurrent and persistent thoughts, impulses, or images that are intrusive and cause severe anxiety or distress. Compulsions refer to repetitive behaviors and rituals (like hand washing, hoarding, ordering, checking) or mental acts (like counting, repeating words silently, avoiding). The obsessions and compulsions also significantly interfere with the teen's normal routine, academic functioning, usual social activities, or relationships."

—from *www.aacap.org/about/glossary/ocd.htm*

The difference between a clutterer and a hoarder, in my observations, is being able to differentiate between what might have some value and garbage. If your teen eats in his room, he may not carry the dirty dishes to the kitchen. That's almost normal. If he saves the half-eaten sandwiches or stockpiles food, that's over the line and may indicate a hoarding disorder.

Kim Arrington Cooper, M.Ed., a family counselor who's worked with a lot of abused children, told me that hoarding could be a sign of abuse. She also told me of an anorexic teen who hoarded. She was torn between fear of not having enough and eating too much and becoming fat. So if your children have begun hoarding, it's not something you should ignore.

## A Clutterer and a Hoarder Went to Lunch

My favorite story to differentiate the two conditions is this. A clutterer and a hoarder go to a fast-food restaurant. The clutterer takes extra ketchup packages, salt and pepper, and napkins because, "they might come in handy later." The hoarder saves the half-eaten sandwich and the box it came in because, "I may run out of food."

## In Conclusion

You've gotten a lot to digest in this chapter. Chances are that your children are normal and don't need to visit a psychologist. Most likely just knowing what's going on in their heads and how to talk to them will help you all live clutter-free lives. But knowing what to look for in their cluttering behavior may help some of you spot some more serious underlying issues early on. Knowledge is power. Use it wisely.

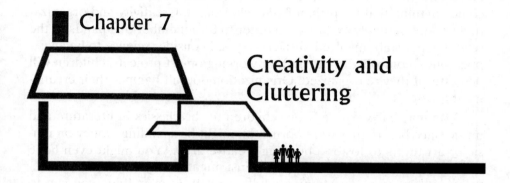

# Chapter 7

# Creativity and Cluttering

*I don't feel that organization stifles creativity.*
*Disorganized kids aren't worse students, they just*
*waste more time and make it harder on themselves.*
*Some disorganized kids spend much of their day*
*rummaging through backpacks.*

—Karen Wiggins, Ph.D.,
school counselor

*Being in the band does teach them some basic skills*
*they need to cope with life. It was something they*
*wanted to do so badly they did well in other ways.*
*Other teachers said a few were disorganized but they*
*got better in all schoolwork. I sat down with them*
*and said, "This has got to change." My success was*
*in having structure. They didn't have a chance to be*
*disorganized.*

—Lee Boyd Montgomery,
retired Texas band director
and member of the
Texas Bandmasters Hall of Fame

Mr. Montgomery, quoted previously, has positively affected the lives of thousands of kids during his long and distinguished career. He hit the nail on the head—if a kid wants to do something badly enough, he'll overcome anything that keeps him from achieving it. Creativity and organization are not mutually exclusive. In order to be a member of a band, on the school paper staff, involved in science (yes, I consider science to be an expression of controlled creativity), or working on art projects, children will do better if they're organized. Organization doesn't hamper their creativity, it focuses it.

You may have exposed your children to the classics in literature and music since before they were born. You might be spending money on music or art tutors to foster a budding creative artist. You might even hope your children become writers. Or you just might want your children to develop into creative, questioning adults, so you do everything you can to encourage their natural inclination to think outside the box. You don't want them to become cogs in the corporate machine like most adults. All this talk about rules and routines runs counter to what you see as creative expression. The one thing you don't want to do is stifle your children.

Good for you! All parents want their children to have a better life than they have. Kids don't always want to follow your plan, but that's their prerogative. Whether you envision an artistic life for them, or one that's more practical and more likely to help them make a living, you want to help them learn to think independently. Even accountants are creative. Some are more creative than they should be, but that's more about ethics than creativity.

## Everyone Is Creative

Everyone has creative traits. Just being a parent brings out creativity. Some people develop the so-called right-brain tendencies more than others. (By the way, a controversial yet enlightening and sometimes debunking book on sinistrality is *The Left-Hander Syndrome*, by Stanley Coren.) Being left-handed doesn't automatically make children more creative or clutterers (I am left-handed), but there does seem to be a preponderance of clutterers who match that description at Clutterless meetings. With informal surveys taken over three years and about 500 respondents, 30 percent of us are lefties. We all think we're more creative than the average bear. About 10 percent of the population is predominately left-handed.

Could it be that we lefties do have a harder time with putting things away because everything operates backward to us?

When I'm talking about "creative" children, I don't mean that all children aren't creative. I mean specifically those who naturally express artistic, writing, or musical abilities. Not every child fits this definition of creative. Some people like thinking inside the box, coloring inside the lines. God knows the world needs both kinds of people.

## Creative Children Relate to Time Differently

Creative children do have some special needs regarding cluttering and not-cluttering. Part of it relates to the creative mind. To a creative child, a project may not be completed in one session. It almost always requires tinkering and tweaking. The creative mind, especially in children, has a hard time correlating time constraints regarding artistic endeavors. (I conducted a thorough discussion of this in *Clutter-Proof Your Business*, if you want to pursue the idea.)

Though there are no guarantees, parents say that less obviously creative, more logic-oriented children seem to be more likely to intuitively understand that when play-time is over, things should get put up. (That doesn't necessarily mean they'll do it, but that they'll understand that it should be done). More apparently creative children will think that only when the project is done, is it time for the paints, crayons, papers, scissors and other paraphernalia to get put away. The creative child isn't being willfully messy. She merely has a different definition of "done." When either type is involved in something that spans more than one day, it's better to make special allowances for the project itself than to impose rigid rules that stifle the creativity.

## Practical Suggestions for Children of All Ages

Here's how to keep the artistic juices flowing and still not have your house look like an artist's loft in the Left Bank district of Paris. Each child should be given a specific area for their creative work. I know that we don't all live in mansions of many rooms (in the physical sense) and this specific area may be part of your living room, so let's develop some practical ways to keep the family rooms looking decent and to accommodate your children's artistic impulses. I also know that we aren't all so rich that we can spend a lot of money on buying specially designed play-area furniture.

## It's Not Over Until It's Put Away

> "We were taught to stop our finger-painting or coloring 10 minutes before playtime was over. Mother insisted that everything be put up, brushes and hands washed, so that we could get ready for dinner on time. That little habit spilled over into schoolwork and, today, into my working life. I've found that spending the last 10 minutes of the day putting things away brings closure."
>
> —Angela, a graphic designer

An important lesson you can teach your children now that will carry forward into their adult working life is to tell them that things need to get put away 10 minutes before playtime's over. Adults need the same 10-minute warning at their offices. Fortunately, adults usually are quite ready to quit playtime at 5:00 or earlier.

Let's say your children like to color in coloring books. They'll need a table to spread the coloring book on and crayons. They'll want to leave the coloring book open to the last page they worked on and the crayons they used out on the table. This is one time you can actually teach them to put things up without making them feel like they're losing their creativity. Say:

> "Crayons live in the crayon box. That's their home, just like your room is your special place. They're happier when they're together when you're not here to keep them company and use them. If you put them up now, you'll be able to find them easier when you want to go back to coloring tomorrow. So that you'll be able to go back to your picture right away tomorrow, let's put a sticky note on the page so that it stands out from the book."

Have a shelf (low enough for the child to reach easily) for the coloring books and crayons. They'll know right where their work of creative genius is and won't be worried about losing their place.

If they're involved in something that requires paints, glitter, cutting and pasting pictures from magazines, or other complicated art activities (and please, please get your left-handers left-handed scissors), you aren't going to get away so easily. These never seem to be finished in one sitting and can drag on forever. At some point, you may want to teach them about time limitations so they'll learn that projects have a start time and a finish time. But if you're dealing with young children, that would be secondary. Learning one habit at a time is plenty.

If it's a school project, the time limit has already been set. Every artist rebels about having a set amount of time to create. I wish my editors would let me take as long as I wanted to write a book. But if they did that, the publisher might expect to take as long as he wanted to write me a check, so it's a trade-off and another of those pesky life lessons.

### You Gotta Have a Place to Create

They're going to need a bigger table for something like this. Try not to call the kitchen or dining-room table into service. That causes too much stress and wasted time when it comes to putting everything away at the end of the day. Instead, designate a table for your children (or each child). If you can't afford a table, a piece of plywood set on top of nonessential furniture or crates works just fine. Your children don't care if you spent $300 or $13 dollars on a table. For them it's the utility that counts, not the form.

Regardless of the type of table, cover it with an old sheet (here's a chance for you to declutter and feel good about making the best use out of something instead of throwing it away), newspapers, or something so they won't have to worry about making a mess. Mess-making is an integral part of artistry and of being a child. The paints and glitter bottles may have come with a little holder to put them in, but if not, an old spice rack works just fine. Those inexpensive plastic trays for kitchen cutlery are perfect also. Brushes live together happily in a drinking glass. There should be two: one for soaking brushes and one for brushes to dry. One thing my father taught me about painting is that brushes should be treated with respect and made ready for the next day before quitting a painting project.

# Let's Use This Opportunity to Learn What's Clutter and What's Not

When the time comes to stop for the day, your children won't want to pick everything up because it'll stop the creative flow or just be too much trouble. That's fine. There are a couple of decluttering chores they should do that will teach them how to determine the value of what's clutter and what's not. The scraps of paper from their cutouts are clutter. Paints and glitter bottles should have their tops or caps put back on, or they'll turn into clutter. Those items can be returned to their trays. Brushes need to be cleaned and set out to dry. If there are big globs of spilled paint, the sheet or newspapers should be trashed. The lesson here is to leave their desk in a neat order so they can start work the next time they go back to the project and not feel overwhelmed by a cluttered mess.

Now, how about you? You don't want this mess to be an obvious eyesore. Whether the work area is in the family room or the children's room, it shouldn't detract from the appearance of neatness. Once a room gets to a certain point of clutterdom, it breeds more clutter and the feeling that it's hopeless to get it back. One Clutterless member coined the phrase "perma-clutter" to describe the stuff that is like the frozen tundra of clutter. Once something has lain in a certain spot long enough, it gets covered with more stuff. You feel like an archeologist when you tackle it—pith helmet optional.

Here's a simple solution: Hide the mess with a room divider. Your children will know their project is there waiting for them and learn a valuable lesson that clutterers have used to break projects down and not have to start over every time they declutter. Sometimes it's better to leave a half-done decluttering project out than to spend a lot of time shuffling piles and stacks into meaningless neatness. Neatly organized clutter is still clutter.

Now you've given your children free creative reign and maintained the appearance of order. What a deal!

## How to Avoid Encouraging the Myth of Cluttering Being a Mark of Creativity

> "We have one or two editors at the paper who can get away with being messy, because they are so good that management cuts them slack. The rest of us can't. We would be fired for being disorganized."
>
> —A reporter for a large
> international newspaper,
> who wishes to remain anonymous

If you let your children clutter because you believe it's a necessary part of being creative, you're laboring under a misconception. We all know a cluttered coworker who gets away with cluttering because so many people believe it's a mark of genius. True, Einstein was a clutterer, but I don't think we should draw a cause and effect conclusion from that.

Don't let the myth of the messy creative genius color your thinking about cluttering and creativity. True, many creative people are messy, but, just like being alcoholic, it's a negative trait that hampers their true creativity. Artists have to know where their paints, brushes, and drawing pads are, or they waste valuable creative juices searching for materials. Writers have to be able to put their hands on inspiring books, articles, and research materials without wasting creative time. Musicians need to keep their strings, reeds, mouthpieces, and music together so they can concentrate on creating melodies. We hear about geniuses with eccentricities, but most artistic types are people who approach their particular branch of artistry in a workmanlike manner. They're the bulk of the ones who make a living at their crafts.

> "I know I'd be a lot more successful if I could overcome my cluttering. It would cut down on the stress of being on the road. It's hard to be creative when you're wondering where your equipment is. Your book, *Stop Clutter From Stealing Your Life*, has helped a lot, but I still have a long way to go."
>
> —Joe King Carrasco,
> "the King of Tex-Mex Rock and Roll"

I'm no artistic genius. I'm a workhorse who gets assignments, does research, and works on a schedule to complete assignments. I'm typical of the great majority of working writers. In order to do what I do, I have to know where the materials I need are. When I was in the throes of my cluttering behavior, I managed to produce 17 nonfiction books, but it took me about three times as long as it should have, because of all the time I wasted looking for research. I had an enabling boss who believed the myth of creativity and cluttering. My mind was cluttered as well, so I had to write perhaps a dozen drafts of works when two or three (okay, four for this

book) would have done for an organized writer. In my newspaper col-
umn-writing days, it took me twice as much work to make deadlines. Thus,
I was working for half-pay.

So one motivator for your children who bring up the supposed cluttered creative genius theory could be that they can stay cluttered and get
paid half as much. They'll either spend more time working than playing,
or enjoying the fruits of their labor. Productive writers like Conrad,
Hemingway, and Asimov turned out impressive bodies of work. And they
were incredibly neat, organized, and focused when it came to their writing.

## Compartmentalization Is the Key

The secret to being decluttered and creative at the same time is com-
partmentalization. Some areas of life don't lend themselves to creativity,
such as driving, taxes, or housework. Housework is, at least, a welcome
break from the stress of all that thinking that goes into decluttering.

Arranging a room can be a creative experience, if approached with
the right attitude. Children of all ages want to have a space of their own.
While the little ones can hardly be expected to emulate interior decorators,
school-age children and teenagers can use their rooms to express themselves.
In fact, one psychiatrist suggested to me that negotiating a license for
children, especially teenagers, to decorate as they see fit will actually aid
in their keeping their rooms neat. Parents need all the tools they can get.
Outwitting your children by letting them have their own way in order to
get yours is perfectly acceptable.

# White Space and Feng Shui

They'll need a little guidance from you at first. While their tendency
will be to cover every inch of their wall space with posters, you can point
out to them that white space between the posters has a value of its own.
Creative use of white space is an art. If they have a nascent interest in feng
shui, encourage it. One of the principles of this oriental philosophy is that
space is an important part of the total effect of our possessions on our
sense of well-being.

Feng shui isn't a science, it's an art. There are those who swear by it
and wouldn't think of living or working in a space that doesn't have feng
shui, and there are those who call it superstition. My view, with children

who want to try it, is to let them. It's not about religion, it's about philosophy. Whatever gets your kids to learn to live uncluttered lives is your ally.

# Turn Their Love of Books and Mementos Into a Creative Expression

Anyone can cram all their books onto a bookcase (well, maybe five or six bookcases). Arranging them so they're in order according to subject or author takes creative skills. Interspersing the bookcase with statues, baseballs, dolls, or other appropriate toys takes real imaginative skills. Leaving toys and clothes on the floor doesn't require any creative skills. Creating clear space and putting those items where they belong is an art. If kids have dolls, coins, stamps, or other items from foreign countries, encourage them to arrange these items by continents or even geopolitical regions (for older kids).

## Make Maps and Globes Part of the Decor

Kids are aware of what's going on in the world. Helping them organize and group foreign items according to the news stories they hear and read can help them understand better and help them overcome stereotyping. Europe is a continent with many different countries and cultures, not just France and Germany. Arab nations are unique, not just Iraq or Iran. By helping them arrange items from different countries according to the continent they're from, they'll learn that there are many parts to the puzzle of humanity.

One of my favorite possessions as a child was a box of minerals from different states. It was arranged alphabetically. My childish mind thought this was the way the states were laid out. I thought Alabama was next to Alaska (a little off) and that Arkansas came next. My parents became aware of my confusion and bought me a wall map and a globe. When I started collecting coins and stamps, these helped me get a sense of the world, which helped me in geography.

## Encourage Creativity in Organizing

Organizing doesn't have to be a boring routine with a lot of preset rules. Stuff doesn't care where it goes. People care. The first rule of living an uncluttered life is that people are more important than stuff. (I know you've heard this from me before, and probably will again. It's important). Your children may not like putting things back into the same places year after year. Let them experiment. An advantage to letting them rearrange their possessions (and if they are really good at it, your living room) is that they might find that everything doesn't fit or look good with the new scheme. Great! What better reasons to get rid of stuff?

There'll be times when you'll want to scream at their "decorating." As long as it's in their own room, back off. It they want to paint the walls purple or put in wild carpeting (and they can pay for the remodeling), let 'em. If they can think of their rooms as apartments they're subletting from you, they'll be more invested in them. Our goal in living an uncluttered life is to make our space personal and warm. For some of us, it means having more possessions around us. If we've created the space, we're more likely to limit the possessions to the ones that match.

So set aside your fears of stifling creativity by teaching not-cluttering behavior. You are, in fact, encouraging it. Way to go, Mom and Dad!

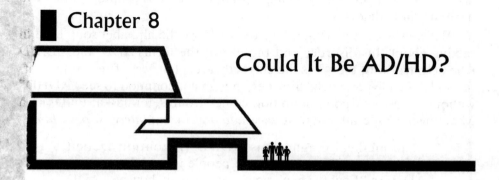

# Chapter 8

## Could It Be AD/HD?

*The most common cause of hyperactivity, distractibility, and/or impulsivity with children, adolescents and adults is anxiety. When you are anxious, you cannot sit still or pay attention.*

—Dr. Larry Silver,
from *Dr. Larry Silver's
Advice to Parents on ADHD*

*What is most important to understand about ADHD children is not simply that they move about too much*—it is that they behave too much.... *Their behavior occurs too quickly, too forcefully, and too easily in situations where other children would have been more inhibited.*

—Russell A. Barkley, Ph.D.,
author of *Taking Charge of ADHD*,
a psychologist, and
past president of the
Attention Deficit Disorder Association

Do you have a kid who's got you running around like a chicken missing a head? Does Dennis the Menace seem like a model child to you? Did your sweet darling just ask Aunt Millie (the rich one) why she's so fat—and smells so bad? Does your kid constantly forget his homework and books and lose stuff in general? You might want to read this chapter—when you have the time, that is.

Before we go any farther, let's try to clarify the alphabet soup used in talking about this disorder and the use of the terms *ADD* and *AD/HD* (the acronym with the "/" is the currently accepted way of referring to attention deficit hyperactivity disorder, though it is common to see "ADHD" without a slash). A good definition comes from Peter Jaska, Ph.D., in a Menninger Clinic interview at *www.add.org/content/interview/peter.htm*:

> "The medical diagnosis is ADHD (Attention Deficit
> Hyperactivity Disorder). Some people use ADD to mean
> ADHD without the hyperactive component, however ADD
> is not an 'official' medical diagnosis. Also many people use
> ADD as a more generic term, to mean all types of ADHD.
> So yes, I agree, it can get confusing sometimes!!"

Just to confuse you more, Dr. Barkley says that children without the hyperactivity component are actually "lethargic, sluggish, or slow moving, compared to other children." His book *Taking Charge of ADHD* should be recommended reading for any parent who wants to know more. It's factual, readable, and addresses the needs of the parents as well as the children. It has sound parenting advice for all children, so read it even if your children aren't AD/HD candidates. Cluttering kids and adults so often have some of the characteristic behaviors of people with AD/HD that his recommendations can help anyone.

This is an important and complicated subject. I could not address it completely in one chapter. While I feel it necessary to impart some brief overview of AD/HD, for the most part, I'm only going to discuss those issues that apply to cluttering and decluttering. There are plenty of good books written entirely on AD/HD, and they are listed in the bibliography.

## Do We All Have a Little ADD?

Most clutterers think they have AD/HD. Most of us don't, but we have a lot in common with folks who do. The good news about this is that the techniques that help AD/HD kids live in a "normal" world also help cluttering kids and adults to declutter. ADD (without the hyperactivity aspect) is an exaggeration of tendencies we all have: being easily bored or distracted, taking risks, being impulsive, not paying attention to details, losing things, speaking without thinking, and so on. How many of you have gotten in trouble with your boss, spouse, or a cop from the last trait? Or any of them?

Did you ever forget an assignment at work, or turn in a report you thought was great but you missed a tiny detail, such as basing everything on 2,000 units of widgets instead of 200,000? If so, welcome to the world of an AD/HD kid, but magnify it by 1,000 (or maybe it's 100,000) times. It's no wonder they're frustrated. People notice their mistakes and comment on them far more often than they do on what they do right. You'd be frustrated if you were in their shoes too.

Whether you, your children, or your spouse have AD/HD, you'll probably recognize some of the symptoms in yourself or your kids and be able to use the solutions in your own family.

An interesting observation about a commonality between AD/HD kids and clutterers, in general, came from Kim Arrington Cooper, M.Ed., a therapist who's worked with lots of AD/HD kids: "Most AD/HD kids are night owls, but they need less sleep." Most clutterers are night owls too. The world discriminates against night people and the world discriminates against AD/HD kids. We both get called lazy, when, in fact, we're just being true to our natures.

## It's a Controversial Condition

Want to make messing with a hornet's nest seem like a lazy summer pastime? Mention AD/HD the next time you're lucky enough to escape to an adult gathering. If you really want to have fun, bring it up on a late-night radio talk show. People are strongly either for or against this disorder.

AD/HD is controversial. Dr. Terrence Early, M.D., a psychiatrist who works with AD/HD children and adults, explained the reasons for the controversy succinctly in an interview:

> "Some diseases are due to a qualitative difference that is either there or isn't (like dead heart tissue following a myocardial infarction), but others are differences in the amount of something (like blood pressure, attention, blood sugar). When a disease is due to a difference in quantity, rather than quality, there is a cutoff established to define the point at which you define a disease (like diastolic blood pressure >90, blood sugar >110, or degree of attention

dysfunction). The cutoff is usually the point at which the variation in the parameter exceeds the point at which symptoms or disability occurs."

There are some people who even doubt the existence of AD/HD as a medical disorder, but because there's so much evidence for it, they seem to be barking up the wrong tree. The general consensus of those who know is that it is more often under-diagnosed than over-diagnosed.

# What Is AD/HD?

Do your kids start to clean up their room, but get distracted and "forget" what they were supposed to be doing? Do they start a project, whether cleaning, decluttering, or schoolwork, and not finish it because they went for a swim in the eddies of related projects they encountered? Do they just burn with activity and cause disruptions in public, home, and school? Do they seem to blurt out what's on their minds without taking the time to think? These could be symptoms of AD/HD. Only your physician knows for sure. If your child is diagnosed with AD/HD, look on the bright side. It just means that he marches to the tune of a different drummer. The other side of this coin is that they're intuitive and very imaginative. They're likely to "know" the solution to something in a flash of inspiration, while the rest of us plod along trying to figure it out.

The highest estimate I could find of children with AD/HD was 10 percent, with about 5 percent being an average consensus. Thus, there is at least a 90-percent chance that your child doesn't have AD/HD. But this chapter is here because we can all learn from their special ways of coping.

Often, a teacher or counselor at school will suggest your child be tested for AD/HD. To find out, your doctor will have to rule out a lot of other possible reasons for your child's attention difficulties. The only way to know for sure is to have a series of tests done by a competent psychiatrist who specializes in AD/HD.

## Rewards Work Better Than Punishment

"Another thing I have found helpful is the A-B-C mnemonic for making a workable household rule. *A* stands for agreement, the initial buy-in to the rule with the child.

It would work something like, 'I make rules for myself to help me remember to do things like pay bills. I don't allow myself to go shopping until I have paid my bills. I thought of a way of making a rule to help us keep the household more livable.' After the agreement, then there is a behavior [*B*] (such as picking up the room at a specified time), or the opposite (failing to pick it up). This leads to *C*, the consequence. Positive behavior leads to getting ice cream, negative behavior leads to no TV, or something like that. The positive consequence is a way of getting buy-in to the rule. The child gets something they otherwise would not get if they abide by the rule, in exchange for losing something if they break the rule."

—Dr, Terrence Early, M.D.

By helping your kid earn rewards for doing "right," you're also helping them gain self-esteem. AD/HD kids get beaten down by the general public and other kids who just don't understand. Others see the difficulties, not the child. Decluttering is a great, obvious way to establish rewards for your kid. It's not too intellectual (oh boy, do we know that!) or conceptual, such as "being a good boy or girl."

Just as I talked earlier about using a "bank account" reward system for all your children, it works especially with AD/HD kids. Dr. Bradley has specific details of a reward system in his book *Yes, Your Teen is Crazy!* His suggestions include:

"Establish a bank account of points or poker chips or whatever you can think of that will work for your kid. Something tangible would seem to work best, as the reward is immediate and visible. For each decluttering activity carried out successfully, award chips or points."

He goes on to explain that it wouldn't hurt to provide visual clues at the same time, such as writing something down in a notebook as she goes through the task. Let her redeem the rewards for something she really wants to do, establishing a higher point value for, say, a week at Disney World, than for getting to stay up half an hour later. Somewhere in between will lie the bulk of the rewards.

One drawback to the bank account idea is that AD/HD kids don't visualize the future as well as others and deferred gratification isn't much of a motivator. By having a number of rewards (let her choose what they are) that are easily and quickly attainable, you can keep her motivated. Remind her of the long-term rewards often.

Rewards don't have much value if they can't also be taken away. But go easy on this. You're trying to build your kid up, not tear her down. If she doesn't do some decluttering chore, take away about half of what she would have gained had she done it. If she does something, but with a bad attitude, only give her half the reward. This can teach her that how we do something is just as important as what we do.

It's important when trying to change anyone's behavior to only concentrate on one thing at a time and to give the new behavior time to sink in. Not-cluttering and decluttering the family room might come first. Because you've got to be there to keep your kid on track, this would be a good time to do a little decluttering of your own! Maybe he'll give you a poker chip for clearing off part of the sofa? Come to think of it, why not do something like that? Make a show of presenting yourself with points or chips for decluttering. That way, you'll get something done and your child will feel like this is a family affair. Now, how many chips you need to get a day at the spa is entirely up to you, but try not to cheat.

Not-cluttering is more conceptual. Tell you child that he'll get rewarded for not leaving his shoes in the dining room. You'll have to pay attention, because rewards, to work with AD/HD kids, need to be given very soon after the action (or in this case, the inaction), or they don't have as much value. Because the shoes aren't in the living room, he must have put them someplace. If you didn't notice that action, ask him where his shoes are, then tell him he's being rewarded for putting them up. That should reassociate the action with the reward.

## Does Your Child Have the Fidgets?

Really, that's what AD/HD was called last century—the fidgets. This could be a classic symptom of AD/HD—hyperactivity. It could also be an expression of other medical or neurological disorders. Or it could be that he's simply anxious or bored. Teachers report that these kids will rock in their seats, swing their legs, play with pencils or hair, or tap their fingers incessantly. Others want to talk incessantly. Again, the more likely culprit is anxiety or boredom.

I was a fidgety kid, but it was a result of being bored to death in grade school and anxious about how dreadful recess was to me. Other kids picked on me because I was a "brain" and rotten at athletics. (You wouldn't know it now, but I was tested at the genius level.) I eventually solved the problem by feigning illness, staying at home, and teaching myself to read from a stack of newspapers and a dictionary at the neighbors' house. These nice old folks were clutterers and had several years' worth of newspapers. I guess there can be advantages to cluttering. I could follow all the previous steps relating to focusing by myself. I mention this because, while I had at least one "symptom" of AD/HD, it wasn't really what was going on.

## Hyperactivity

> "Your insides are gong 5,000 miles per hour and your feet are glued to the floor."
>
> —Kim A. Cooper M.Ed.,
> describing what it's like to have AD/HD

Ah, this is what most often comes to mind when we think of AD/HD kids. I'd like to say that we could channel this extra energy into decluttering. After all, it's kind of like having the Ajax tornado. Wouldn't it be nice to put it to work for you? I'd like to, but can't. If you come up with any ideas on this, I'd love to hear them.

Hyperactivity is activity without focus and takes a lot of effort on your part to help your child to act appropriately. Medication can control most of these behaviors, but don't forget the behavioral aspects. Rewards for good behavior help a lot. Getting angry with them (though this is tough not to do when you're frustrated) doesn't.

Praise your kid for *not* acting out in the store or at school. Be prepared. Talk to your kid before you go to the store, church, or anyone's house. Let him know that he's expected to stay close to you and not run around or ask a million questions (well, maybe the last part is too tough for any kid, but give it a shot). Let him know he'll be disciplined if he does act up and be prepared to do so. Time-outs are good, and, if you can find a relatively unexciting spot in the store (sock departments and vegetable bins have always bored me), take him there. At home, a quiet corner with no distractions is good.

One thing a teacher told me is that AD/HD kids may be very well behaved in school, but when they get home become rambunctious. If this is happening in your house, discuss changing the dosage of medication with your doctor.

## Is Your Kid in a Different Time Zone, or Just Zoned Out?

Kids, in general, are likely to know when their favorite shows on TV start. They're less likely to be ready to leave for school on time. If they're consistently unaware of time constraints, that's an AD/HD trait. These folks (and clutterers in general) seem to operate on a different clock than the rest of the world. If your kid loses track of time because of hyperfocusing, or getting so involved in something that he loses track of time on a regular basis, it could be a sign of AD/HD. But don't jump the gun. Everyone hyperfocuses from time to time. Haven't you gotten so involved in something that you "didn't know where the time went"?

## Watch the Watch

One way to help kids understand time is to get them a watch that's cool and does other things than tell local time. My father gave me a watch that told time in several world time zones, and it was a constant source of entertainment for me. Something like that could help keep the attention of an AD/HD child focused on time because it's not boring like a regular watch.

Another way is to give them warnings about the passage of time. AD/HD kids don't have as clear-cut a concept of the future as others. Tell your child something such as, "Okay, Juan, we're going to get ready for dinner (or clean up this room) in 10 minutes." Because kids of all ages and types have a way of tuning out their parents, it's a good idea to have him look at you when you're speaking, and to repeat back to you what you just said. An "Uh-huh," doesn't cut it. For AD/HD kids, in particular, it's a good idea to have him turn down the TV or stereo in order to listen to you.

## It's About Time

Instead of setting definite times for leaving for school, activities, and so on, set "about" times. The idea is not to add 15 minutes or some finite number to everything, but to make events happen an indefinite number of minutes earlier. "We leave for school at about 7:20," which is, in reality, about 7:18 or 7:12 or something earlier than the actual time. This way, they have a goal to shoot for, but it's flexible.

Reward your children for being early. Teach them to use the "extra" time they get to read, study, or do something they enjoy. The very best thing you can do for any kid, but especially for those with AD/HD, is to reinforce their positive behavior. These kids get called on the carpet for acting out so much that their self-esteem tends to sink lower than the stock market. Give them a boost.

## AD/HD Kids Are Drawn to Fun Things

Aren't we all! They also like physical activities better than passive ones. That's a good thing! They're less likely to want to waste their time with TV. Now we just need to channel that into positive physical activities. Remember the clutter dance? It will work well with them. Remember the treasure hunt aspect of decluttering? Now you've got the ticket. Do whatever you can to make decluttering a fun activity, and you'll be rewarded more from your AD/HD kid than even your other kids.

Another strategy that will help them to perform decluttering activities is to time them to happen within the period of peak medication effect.

## Internal Chatter

Kids with AD/HD actually concentrate better when there's noise around them. It helps them drown out the internal chatter going on in their heads. Let them play their music while they study. For your own sake, buy them earphones, because one thing that will probably never change is that a kid's idea of "a reasonable volume" will be closer to an adult's idea of "that's so loud I can't think." Of course, the issue of premature deafness comes into play, but you've probably already had that talk with your kids. That is, if it isn't too late and they can still hear you.

If they try to declutter in a quiet environment, they'll very quickly get distracted. Music soothes the savage clutterer.

They may also be auditory learners, so when they put something away, encourage them to say what it is and where they're putting it. This creates a link in their brain so that they can find it again.

## Hyperfocusing

If you've ever gotten so wrapped up in what you were doing that you completely forgot about the outside world, you have hyperfocused. It's normal for kids to get so involved in a game, or even studying, that they're unaware of what's going on around them. This is good. If they're tuning you out when you call them to bed, but can hear the telephone ringing or the Instant Messenger alarm on their computer, then that's another issue.

This can be a great trait if used in decluttering. Encourage it. Even if it seems like your kid is concentrating on something less important than you think he should, leave him alone. Any decluttering is better than no decluttering.

## Long-term? What's That?

> "Because of the neurological deficit in the ability to inhibit behavior, people with ADHD not only do not see what lies ahead as well as others, but *cannot* do so as well as others. In essence, holding them responsible for their problem with anticipating and planning for the future is like holding the deaf person responsible for not hearing us or the blind person accountable for not seeing us—it is ridiculous and serves no constructive social purpose."
>
> —Dr. Michael Bradley,
> from *Yes, Your Teen Is Crazy!*

It's like two different types of speculators. Long-term investors have a vision of where they want to be in 10 years or 20 years. Options traders have a hard time seeing beyond the next few hours, if that long. They're also aware that time is a wasting asset in options. The longer they hold something, the less the time value will be worth. I was an options trader. Long-term never interested me. It was boring. And in a sense, who knew what the future held? So there's something to be said for the AD/HD view of things. Keep the day-to-day tasks up, and the future will take care of itself.

## Attention Span

Kids with AD/HD are behind in their development in this area. It's been estimated that they are often years behind in being able to pay attention to details and boring tasks (such as decluttering, for instance). Thus your 11-year-old with AD/HD may be as focused as her 7-year-old brother.

You'll probably have to help them declutter their rooms, or you'll both grow old before it gets done. Your job isn't to do it for them, but to help them keep from getting distracted. Sending them off to their room to declutter it is like sending a soldier with no sense of direction into the jungle alone, to paraphrase an old Judy Collins song I've always identified with. Get in the trenches with them, Captain.

If your child is very easily distracted and unable to tune out what's going on around him, this could be a valid warning sign of AD/HD. Let's say you ask your child to clean up his room, and later find him having played with half a dozen toys instead. He could be just acting willful (oppositional defiant disorder), avoiding (procrastinating), or displaying a symptom of AD/HD. If he can't seem to concentrate when there's the least bit of distraction (TV or radio in another room, someone walking into a room, or visually distracting objects vying for his attention), that's more likely a sign of the possibility of AD/HD.

One of the techniques suggested by AD/HD advocates is *turning up* the distractions so that the child can concentrate. It then becomes "white noise" and helps the kid pay attention. It seems to work for both children and adults!

Clutterers and individuals with AD/HD often get sidetracked and don't finish their projects. The psychological term for being able to focus is "attending." Not attending isn't intentional, it's just that so much vies for their attention. Use this to your and your kid's advantage. Make decluttering chores short and sweet. Well, the sweet part may be a stretch, but short is good. While all decluttering tasks should be broken down into smaller chunks, it's especially true for AD/HD kids. Putting away their shoes is one specific task. Congratulate them on that. Then move to the socks, and so on. A few minutes on each task may be all they can handle. Take a lot of breaks. Do the same thing with schoolwork. A chapter in a book may be a lot. Reading a couple of paragraphs, then taking a break to write down what they just read, could help them get through assignments.

## Avoidance Is Most Likely the Culprit

Children don't have a monopoly on this psychological trait. If your child can pick something she wants to do (watch TV, play with toys, play a video game) but doesn't want to quit it to do something she'd rather not do (make her bed, put away her toys), then she (or you) can't blame this AD/HD trait. You've both learned the wonderful value of procrastinating.

Procrastinating can overcome the second and third steps to completing a project. We all do this to some degree. Clutterers especially overuse this weapon in their arsenal of reasons not to declutter. For children and adults, decluttering is boooorrrrrinnng. Even the relatively mindless activity of watching TV is preferable to decluttering. Did you know that studies have shown that brain activity while watching TV is closer to that of being asleep than anything else we can do while awake? Okay, I haven't been to your weekly company bored (I mean board) meeting, so maybe you know another one. Video games and reading at least require some involvement of the brain, so if your child would rather play video games than watch most TV (except educational programs), God bless him.

To avoid avoidance, remember the rewards system and making decluttering fun. And there's always the technique of suggesting some other activity that he'd rather avoid more than decluttering if he doesn't want to do the decluttering.

### Mom, I Just Forgot!

Help them to learn things the way they remember. Writing down the tasks they need to accomplish is a big help. So are posters with assigned chores and decluttering activities. If they are mainly auditory, have them say what they are going to do out loud. Ask them to repeat what you just said. They could carry a tape recorder to play back to remind themselves of what they're supposed to be doing. If they're mainly visual learners, keep the places where they put stuff in sight and brightly colored. If they're tactilely oriented, make sure they feel what they are putting away and maybe pat it when it is done. If they're intellectual, encourage them to make mental relationships to their items by category, or something they've studied. The same principles go for schoolwork.

## School and Learning

A small but very practical thing that can help ease the stress of AD/HD kids at school is a lock with a key. Really. It might make your AD/HD child feel better to know that teachers have told me that even so-called "normal" kids have difficulty with combination locks, too. If you want, you can even tell them that one of the greatest authors (me) you've read (or however you want to stretch the truth) had so much trouble with combination locks that he practically has a phobia about them.

> "Children with disabilities often can't use a combination lock, so ask the school to let them use a key lock."
>
> —Karen Wiggins, Ph.D.,
> school counselor

Instead of their having different notebooks for different subjects, get them one notebook with colored dividers for different subjects. Five dividers ought to do the trick. Don't sweat that it may not last the entire year. You can always buy another one, and keeping the first part of the year in a designated space will be a good lesson for your child.

Backpacks are standard equipment for kids and school. But it's easy to confuse the different compartments, even if there are only two. Taping the name of what goes into each compartment on the outside will encourage snide comments from the other kids, but you can put them on the inside to help your child remember. On the outside, put differen colored stickers, or even better, stickers of his favorite cartoon characters. Leave it to him to decide what subject or group of items the Hulk represents.

AD/HD kids are perceived as "slow," when in fact they are too fast at processing information. According to Kim Cooper, M.Ed.:

> "They can learn and retain at up to 1,000 to 1,500 words a minute. By speeding up the information flow, they're forced to focus. The plus is they enjoy it at those speeds. Generally we read for pleasure at 600 wpm, and reading for learning is lower than that. A teacher generally talks at 200 words per minute. So what you have—in the child's perception—is a bored and restless kid trying to listen and retain information that is being delivered in what feels like slow motion. Children that are visual, auditory, and kinesthetic in learning style (most all ADHD kids) have different needs for repetition rates and speed of information."

That's where medication comes into play. It slows them down to fit in with us "normal" but slow people. Any learning activity you can tie in with computers will help them learn and retain information at a pace closer to theirs.

Dr. Russell A. Barkley, Ph.D., in his book *Taking Charge of ADHD*, emphasizes that, "The single most important ingredient in your ADHD child's success at school is your child's teacher."

## Teacher, Teacher

Today, teachers are more aware of AD/HD kids and are supposed to make reasonable accommodations for them. Most teachers will. There are some who are still prejudiced or feel they just don't have the time to give a few kids special attention. I'm sorry, but that's part of their job. If you feel like your child is being discriminated against, contact the administration. If you can't work it out, contact the Attention Deficit Disorder Association at *www.add.org*, or at:

> ADDA
> 1788 Second Street
> Suite 200, Highland Park, IL 60035
> Phone: 847-432-ADDA (to leave a message)
> Fax: 847-432-5874

"For kids with AD/HD or learning disabilities, let the teachers know who they are. Teachers are very good about modifying the classroom setting for them. At school they are seated up near the front or with teacher proximity. Teachers can give them a tap on the desk or some other signal to keep them focused. They might use red cards or green cards as a silent signal for them. Those with learning disabilities are placed in the least restricted environment. They often allow them to stand up beside their desk and work. They give them shortened assignments, time to take a short break, or let them stop to get up. Medication often wears off when the kid gets home, so they'll be better behaved at school than at home."

—Karen Wiggins, Ph.D.,
school counselor

The solution for the medication issue should be discussed with your physician. Dr. Terrence Early, M.D., explains that "this worsening is due to rebound, and that the change in meds might be a second dose later in the day." But, this should only be done on the advice of your own doctor.

Good teachers establish nonverbal signals to help these children focus and have them sit in the front of the class and away from the hall where the passersby might distract them. Let your child's teacher know if your kid has been diagnosed. To keep your AD/HD child interested in school (they probably have intuited what's next long before the other kids), help them with their homework. If your kid is light-years ahead of the other students, encourage them to research more about the subject.

I read too fast as a child. I'd finish assignments in about a quarter of the time it took the other students. In those unenlightened days, I got a strap to the hand from Sister Mary Merciless for my "disruptive behavior." It worked. I read a lot slower today.

One "advantage" to your child being diagnosed with a learning disability of any kind is that it affords them special treatment at school. Among other things, it allows them an unlimited amount of time to take the SAT and other tests. When you and I were growing up, schools didn't want to deal with special kids. Now, in fact, some teachers have told me (privately) that the administration welcomes special students. Schools look better to their governing agencies if they have a higher number of "learning challenged" students. And, as with almost everything, there's a darker side to having children diagnosed with some sort of medical condition. One teacher confided to me that her students bragged about their contribution to the family's financial condition because, "My mommy gets 'crazy money' for me."

The kids could only have heard that terminology from their parents. Please, don't set up a negative stereotype. "Crazy," "dummy," and "AD/HD" should never be in the same sentence.

## Homeschooling

Many parents with AD/HD kids choose this alternative because they can give their kids individual attention and adjust the learning schedule to fit their children's unique abilities. The previous suggestions apply, but you have more latitude, such as allowing more freedom of movement and the ability to try teaching methods designed specifically for AD/HD kids. Online groups such as at *http://pinksunrise.com/form1.htm* have a lot of different viewpoints in this aspect.

One mom who homeschools her AD/HD boy told me that she breaks tasks into smaller chunks than is possible at a regular school and can be innovative. A drawback to homeschooling is that there is less opportunity for social interaction, so she enrolls her son in community sports and other events to be around other children.

Clutter-wise, homeschooling is more of a challenge, because you are the teacher and have to have more materials to organize yourself, and, because all projects get done at home, there's more clutter in general.

> "I decided to homeschool Aaron because I just didn't feel he was getting the attention he deserved at the local public school. I learned a lot about teaching methods before I took this on and am still learning. Part of our program is that we make decluttering part of the lessons. Things have to be put up and organized before we close a subject. I think it's working because Aaron will remind me when I forget to put my own materials away. I think it's helped, in that respect."
>
> —Sylvia,
> a single mom
> with an AD/HD kid

What this mother did was implement decluttering as part of the process of learning. It's done wonders for her, as well as for her son. But, she admits, "I'm lucky because I can arrange my schedule to make this work. It's created a lot more work for me, but I wouldn't trade a minute of it."

# Computers

They'll do well at adapting to computers, because of the stimulation. Get them a noisy keyboard that goes "click, click, click," instead of one that goes "nothing, nothing, maybe a little squeak, nothing." I think it would be a good idea to find a drawing program or even one of those home-design programs so they can set up a virtual room and put things away. This could help them in the real world.

# Noise

With their natural distractibility, the more things they have vying for their attention in their room, the more distracted they'll be. When it comes to studying, make sure their study area has absolutely nothing that doesn't relate to the project at hand. For some AD/HD individuals, turning UP the noise level helps them concentrate. The secondary noise becomes "white noise" drowning out extraneous thoughts. Non-AD/HD kids may claim the same thing. The only way to find out is to try it. If they can turn in good assignments, or answer questions you put to them about what they just studied, then whatever they're doing is working.

How high is "up"? About half the volume of what kids think is normal. It was true in our day and it's true today. I guess I've attained fuddy-duddy status. Kids want their music loud. You want to enjoy your home. Don't let your kids manipulate you by turning their music so loud that it shakes the walls or rattles the dishes in the cupboard. That's not compensating. That's accepting rudeness. Loud music is noise clutter and contributes to mental clutter for most kids.

# I Gotta Move!

If your AD/HD child seems to have to get up and go to the bathroom, get a drink of water, or just walk around, let him, within reason. Encourage him to walk over and put things up or engage in some movement during his decluttering. It will help keep him going.

# I Don't Want to Drug My Children

Some people resist getting treatment for their AD/HD kids, because they are afraid of "drugging" them. The common medicines used are Ritalin, Dexedrine, and Adderall (amphetamines). Yes, they are speed. Yes, they should be avoided by normal kids and adults. And yes, they help kids and adults diagnosed with AD/HD.

"The best evidence on the study is the recent MTA study, which compared Ritalin, behavior therapy, and the combination in a large cohort of ADHD kids for 14 months. The upshot was that the best results were seen in the two groups that used stimulants, and the addition of behavior therapy did not seem to offer much over stimulants in terms of better symptom control, quality of life, etc.

"Probably one of the most effective things that a parent can do with an ADHD kid who clutters is to help them stay on an effective dose of stimulants. These drugs have been used since 1937 and are very safe and effective. They have been shown to lower the risk of later substance abuse and improve self-esteem.

"There is a lot of misinformation going around about them, much of which is promoted by the Scientologists. This is not to say that behavior therapy is not very important, only that stimulants have been shown to be more effective and are at this point a cornerstone of effective treatment for the more severely symptomatic patients. There is a broad public misconception that is based on absolutely no data that stimulants are somehow bad for kids with ADHD, and the opposite is true. The adults I see often tell me that recognizing and getting treatment for their ADD turns their life around."

—Dr. Terrence Early, M.D.

## Don't Forget Yourself!

Raising a child with AD/HD is tough—even tougher than raising a child without it. If you get burned out, you're not going to do her, or yourself, any good. Arrange to take some time off, either by yourself or with your spouse, if you can get someone understanding to take your child for a weekend or even a day. If you can, just get away for a few hours and go to the beach, to a day spa, for a walk in the woods, to a museum, or even for a stroll in the park. Just go somewhere.

Just being able to talk to someone who understands, or even a good friend who might not understand what you're going through, but can listen without interrupting and telling you how you "should" do things, helps a lot. You are not alone. But you might feel that way. You don't have to. Join a support group.

Support groups work absolute wonders. The most well-known is CHADD, ("Children and Adults With Attention-Deficit/Hyperactivity Disorder"). The organization's Website is *www.chad.org*. They have groups nationwide. If there's not one near you, start one! Starting a group will help you far more than you think. Somebody has to do it. Another link to support groups for AD/HD and other issues is *http://add.miningco.com/library/blsupportmain.htm*.

Online groups include "Moms of ADHD Kids" on Yahoo; *http://messageboards.ivillage.com/iv-psaddchild*, on iVillage; and another is run by Eileen Bailey at *http://add.miningco.com/gi/dynamic/offsite.htm?site=http://www.addhelpline.org*.

## If You Want to Know More

Read all you can and keep up with new research. I happed to like a couple of classics: *You Mean I'm Not Lazy, Stupid or Crazy?!* by Kate Kelly and Peggy Ramundo (Simon & Schuster, New York, 1996) and *Driven to Distraction* by Edward M. Hallowell, M.D. (Touchstone Books, 1995). For yourself, you might like *ADD in the Workplace* by Kathleen G. Nadeau, Ph.D. (Brunner/Mazel Publishers, 1997).

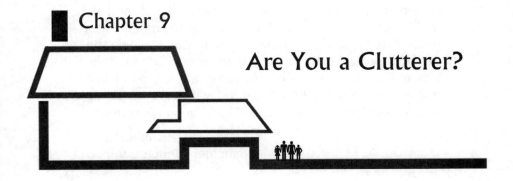

# Chapter 9

# Are You a Clutterer?

*Darlene and I had another big fight about her leaving her stuff in the living room. It ended with her shouting at me, "Mom, how can you expect me to pick up after myself when it won't make any difference? There's so much of your mess around that I don't think it would make any difference if I was a neat freak. I'm ashamed to have my friends come over to this pigsty." Her words hurt, more so because they were true. After she left, I looked around and had to admit that she was right. I cried. I've always been a little messy, but it got out of control after her Dad left. I just feel so overwhelmed that I don't know where to start. I've tried to get organized and it never lasted. I just don't know what to do.*

—Mary Jane, a single mom

That was a sad story, but it shows several facts about cluttering and teaching our children not to clutter. The whole premise of this book is that cluttering is much less about the stuff than about the reasons the stuff has taken control. It's common for someone to be either neat or at least relatively neat most of their life, then begin to clutter after a traumatic life event. This could be a divorce, death of a loved one, or even the loss of a job.

"When my parents separated, the cluttering peaked. I shared a room with my sister who was a clutterer like Mom. Until middle school, she was indifferent to it. By the time we were around 10, 11, or 12, my mom wanted to start cleaning stuff out of the room, baby toys etc. It never worked out. There was never any real action. In some ways, I don't take responsibility for cluttering even today. If leave my clothes on the floor, no one will notice. Then I get away with it."

—Kimberly,
daughter of a clutterer

### A Self-Help Test

1. Do you feel overwhelmed by your clutter?

2. Have you tried to "clean up" or "organize" repeatedly, with no lasting results? Do you feel like, "What's the use, if it will just get messed up again?"

3. Are you ashamed to have guests in your home?

4. Do you feel more confused in your home than in the outside world?

5. Do you buy more of everything because "you never know when you will run out"?

6. Do you have more than one of books, software, clothing, and so on, because you can't find what you already own?

7. Has your spouse or partner expressed dismay about the way you live?

8. Do you hold onto broken items because "they might come in handy someday" or "I'm going to fix them someday"?

9. Do you hold onto relationships that do not serve you, saying, "This is the best I can do"?

10. Do you feel like there will never be enough for you?

11. Do you believe that you do not deserve any better than what you have?

12. Do you feel more "lack" than prosperity in your life?

13. Do you want to change these things?

This test is based on years of working with clutterers. While everyone occasionally experiences some of these situations, if they're your constant companions, there's a good chance you're a clutterer. If you answered yes to any of them, you might want to read the rest of this chapter, and the Appendix, with the "Promises for Clutterers."

## "Do as I Do" Doesn't Do It

We can't teach our children values we don't have. It's like when my dad was telling me not to smoke or drink, while sucking on a Camel and guzzling tequila. While I certainly didn't want to emulate him, I wasn't about to take advice from someone who could talk the talk, but not walk the walk. Most people exhibit behaviors that are at odds with the way they see themselves to some extent, because we set up impossibly high standards, such as being law-abiding all the time, then speeding on the freeway. Nobody's perfect. Not even you.

Kids want to model themselves after their parents. When a parent has behaviors that they don't want the kids to model, such as cluttering, smoking, or drinking, they need to communicate to their kids that they are not perfect, but that doesn't mean the kids can't avoid those behaviors.

If you're a clutterer, give your kids a break for a short time. If you'll spend some time working on your own cluttering habits, it'll pay big dividends later. If you keep at your children for their cluttering, they'll only think you're a hypocrite and either ignore you or resent you. As you get your own house in order (literally in this case), you'll see that they will notice the change in you and be more receptive. You won't declutter the whole house. Just get started.

Once you've gotten a start on what's going on with you, you could come clean (okay, I couldn't resist the pun) with them and admit that you've got a problem. Ask for their help. Can you imagine how this will make your young children feel? They love to help their parents. School-age kids will see that this could have payoffs for them, as they won't have to be ashamed to invite their friends over.

> "There was a lot of tension in our house. Mom had some of the same feelings. Why is all this stuff around? I was less sensitive when I was young. At about middle school, I became acutely aware that this type of house was not the norm."
>
> —Maria,
> daughter of a clutterer

Teenagers, well, it's a toss-up. Some will be honored that you, an adult, are asking for help and be great allies. If you're already having problems with them for being disrespectful, it could go either way. They could be acting that way to express their independence from you and define their own boundaries. They might see this openness of your admitting you have a problem and aren't the all-knowing authority figure as an opportunity to communicate. If their minds are working (always a gamble with teens) that day, they'll pitch in. If they're too cool for you, or already devising new strategies to push your buttons, it'll just be another arrow in their quiver. But you don't have a lot to lose. You know your kids. If at all possible, enlist them as foot soldiers in your battles with clutter.

## If Quick Fixes Worked, You Wouldn't Be Reading This

I do not offer quick fixes or simple 10-step programs to free yourself from cluttering. You have to want to change, and then be willing to work on some inside issues—emotional and psychological. This is hard. For a clutterer to change, she has to grow emotionally. Growth is hardly ever quick and easy, but slow and steady growth lasts. Your relationships with your spouse and with your children will become better, more fulfilling. In the process of learning how to permanently declutter, you'll learn how to free yourself from the negative pall that cluttering casts on a family. Isn't that a lot more valuable than "10 easy steps to getting organized"?

> "Parents want children to know the best of them. Like with alcoholism—when a child is growing up and understands

the problem, they can let go of the personal guilt about it. I didn't feel like the cluttering was my fault, but felt like I didn't help. I was hard on my mom for it, and that didn't help her. I called it the dull roar underneath."

—Ron,
son of a clutterer

## Now for Some Positive News

So what can you do to help your children and yourself? First of all, look on the positive side. You have a great motivation for learning how to not-clutter—the effect it has on your children. I know that all the self-help books and 10-step programs insist that we should change for ourselves and not for another person, but I figure that we should take our motivation where we can find it. One clutterer I know was motivated to make significant changes in her accumulation of stuff because she wanted to travel and live in an RV. As frightening as the prospect of getting rid of all her stuff was, the motivation of new freedom was stronger. She did it! Another woman, whose story is in this book, was motivated to declutter and stay that way because she wanted her niece to come over and visit. I know families who changed from cluttering families to not-cluttering families, because they wanted their kids to be able to invite other children over for play dates. It's hard to change a lifetime of cluttering habits, just like it's hard to lose weight, stop smoking or drinking, or eliminate any other undesirable traits, but it is being done by thousands of people every day. Why not you?

## Are You Cluttering *at* Someone?

Divorce, death, and job loss affect different people different ways, but it's common to be angry or depressed, with a little anxiety thrown into the mix. All of these emotions can be expressed more safely through cluttering than other means. That doesn't mean it's healthy, it's just the way it is. Oh, yeah, let's not forget that demon of control that's always lurking in our mounds of clutter.

This is how it works: You can't really express your feelings that you're angry with someone for dying on you; murdering ex-spouses is frowned upon; fantasies of gunning down your former boss and coworkers, while not completely unheard of, are not considered acceptable behavior. However, in the privacy of your own home, you can throw stuff willy-nilly, wherever you want, and "show them" that you're in control. You may not have much control of what's going on in your life, but you sure as heck have control over inanimate objects.

It's a fool's game, really. You clutter—you get anxious. You clutter—you get overwhelmed. You clutter—you lose. The worst conundrum is that by apparently expressing control over those inanimate objects, you're giving them the power to control you. Now, is that self-defeating behavior or what?

## So What Are We Going to Do About It?

"We" is the operative word here. You've been ignoring your clutter for a long time. You've felt like you're alone. And alone with your clutter is a terrible place to be. I know. I am a reformed clutterer myself and have proven that we can change once we understand what it is we need to change. I didn't do this alone. No book taught me (seriously, when I started my journey of learning to not-clutter, there were no books like mine that addressed the core reasons why we clutter. Organizing books just don't cut it—not for real clutterers). I learned a new way of life with the help of others just like me. There are support groups for darn near everything today, because they work. We clutterers have one: Clutterless Recovery Groups (*www.clutterless.org*). They're a 501(c)(3) nonprofit group. If there's a meeting near you, go. You'll find a safe place to talk about what's really going on with your cluttering behavior with people who understand. If you want information about their services or starting a meeting, send a 9 x 12-inch return envelope with $.83 postage ($5 donation requested to defray expenses) to:

> Clutterless Recovery Groups
> 1714 54th Street, Ste. B
> Galveston, TX 77551-4717

Talking to friends or spouses who don't understand only causes hurt feelings. However, a nonjudgmental friend can help.

Hiring a professional organizer won't solve the problem, because, as good as they are at what they do, their job is not to help you work through your emotions. An organizer can help you organize, which is a component of decluttering, but unless you're already on the road to making the fundamental changes required to modify your behavior, you'll be back where you started in a few months, if it takes that long. Once you've started dealing with the core issues of cluttering, an organizer can help you with the mechanics of staying organized.

Not everyone likes groups. Some people, given the tools in this book, will be able to turn their cluttering lives around. But sometimes it is a lot easier to get outside help, be it from a support group (and you may need support about the real issues such as divorce, death, or unemployment) or a therapist. Cluttering is a symptom. It is not a cause.

## First, Figure out What's Going On

Before you start to pick up the mess you already have, mess some more! But this time, try to be aware of your thoughts and emotions. As you throw that dress on the floor or chair instead of the laundry hamper, ask yourself what's going on. Who are you upset with? Does the dress remind you that you have to wear it to work at a job you hate or go on interviews that seem pointless? Do you feel it makes you look bad? Have you gained weight since the divorce, death, or just because you're too tired with all the other stresses in your life to exercise? Or is the dress just a dress, and you're too tired to walk it over to the hamper or closet?

When you leave stuff in the living room, notice yourself dropping it. Intellectually, you know that putting it away doesn't take that much time, so don't use the excuse that you don't have time to put it away. That dog won't hunt. Do you subconsciously tell yourself something such as, *"It's my house and I'll do what I want"*? Or, if you have a spouse or partner, are you making some kind of control statement to him or her? Do you expect your significant other to pick it up?

Was your mother or father excessively neat? Was your own childhood filled with a sense of being controlled? Are you expressing your adulthood and freedom from them by breaking the rules they crammed down your throat? Serious stuff, but if this is going on in you 20 years later, then you can understand why the same sort of thoughts might be filling *your* children's minds. Rebellion is part of human nature. Cluttering is an easy but lousy way of expressing it.

## Sample Clutter Log

| Day | What I Cluttered With | How It Felt | What Emotions Are Attached? |
|---|---|---|---|
| Monday | Work Dress, Shirt. | I'll show them. | Anger. Resentment. Control. |
| Tuesday | Newspapers. | There's never enough time. | Fear of missing something, or not knowing something. Need to clip articles for others—being needed. |
| Wednesday | Mail. | Not enough time. | Fear of making a decision. Fear of not being able to pay bills. |
| Thursday | Magazines. | Procrastination. | The perfect recipe is in this magazine. The perfect self-help or weight-loss program is in here. I want to be perfect. |
| Friday | Catalogs. | I'll get it later. Procrastination. | I should reward myself with something I want. This catalog is an escape for me. |
| Saturday | Clothes. | I'll show them. No one else around here picks up. | Anger. Resentment. Control. |
| Sunday | Saved church bulletin. Sunday newspaper. | Not enough time. Important information I'll need. | Fear of not knowing everything. Need to help others by clipping articles, volunteering. |

Maybe you just had a bad day. Work was a bear, traffic a nightmare, and your children were throwing tantrums all day. Well, you'll show them, won't you?

Keep a log of what went through your mind as you did each cluttering action (assuming you can find a pen and a small notebook to write them down in). Do this for a week. I bet you'll see a pattern emerge.

The entries in the Sample Clutter Log on page 122 are just examples. Your reasons may be different, but these are pretty common. Right now, let's get one thing straight. You're right—you don't have enough time. You can't read all the information that comes at you. You don't have enough time to use all those recipes. So why do we keep them? Read on, dear friend.

## Now That We Know Where We Are, Let's Go Somewhere Else

Armed with this self-knowledge, the next time you start to clutter, call on your adult self to correct the rebellious child within. It isn't going to be easy. Changing never is. Learning to not-clutter is easier than decluttering. The toughest part of decluttering is making decisions. "What am I going to do with this? Where does it go? Is it important? Will I need it later? Maybe I can fix it. Maybe I better keep it, just in case. I'll just put it over here on this inviting pile until I have time to decide." And so on.

When we're dealing with something that hasn't taken root and grown into our "perma-clutter," we don't have as many decisions to make. As you start to toss something, mentally grab your hand and stop yourself. Call on your rational mind. "You know, throwing this on the cluttered coffee table isn't going to get back at any of those louses I'm angry with. It's a lot less trouble to put it away (or throw it away or recycle it) right now than to deal with it later. By golly, I think I'll put it up!"

## Watch out for the Shadow!

> "The Shadow cannot be eliminated. It is the ever-present dark brother or sister. Whenever we fail to see where it stands, there is likely to be trouble afoot. For then it is certain to be standing behind us. The adequate question therefore never is: Have I a shadow problem? Have I a negative side? But rather: Where does it happen to be right now? When we cannot see it, it is time to beware! And it is helpful to remember Jung's formulation that a complex is not

pathological per se. It becomes pathological only when we assume that we do not have it; because then IT HAS US!"

—Dr. Edward C. Whitmont, from
*www.shadowdance.com/quotes/morequotes.html*

Congratulations! You've made a big, important, first step. Now comes the fun part. Congratulate yourself. Don't let your critical mind kick in and say, *"Big deal. It's only one thing. You've got a mountain of clutter. This won't make any difference at all."* That's really your Shadow Self, your limiting self, talking. For more on what the Shadow Self is and how it relates to cluttering, go to the Clutterless Website (*www.clutterless.org*) or my deceptively-titled book *Clutter-Proof Your Business,* which has a lot of psychology for living life in it. Essentially, the Shadow Self is our dark self that wants to hold us down and tells us that we are failures. If we stuff emotions such as anger, resentment, jealousy, or other socially unacceptable emotions, they don't really go away. They coexist within us. For clutterers, we express our Shadow Self in our cluttering. I guess that's better than going postal, but we should still seek to improve it.

Several psychologists deal extensively with Shadow work, notably Jung; David Richo; Dr. Edward C. Whitmont; W. Brugh Joy, M.D., a teacher of Heart Centered Transformation and Spiritual Enlightenment (*www.brughjoy.com*); and others. We all have several Shadow Selves, and fortunately, the cluttering one is the easiest to work on. We don't defeat our Shadow Self, we merely take away its power. We don't deny it, but we learn to coexist with it. That which we repress shows up in other forms. The book, *Meeting the Shadow: The Hidden Power of the Dark Side of Human Nature*, edited by Connie Zweig and Jeremiah Abrams, is a magnificent compilation of articles on the Shadow Self by many experts, including Dr. Carl Jung. When you're ready to work in this area, you'll find it fascinating and rewarding.

## Fear Is the Enemy

While control is behind most cluttering, behind that is fear. We fear that we'll make mistakes and throw out something we really need. We fear that we can't make perfect decisions, so it's easier to make none. We fear discarding some items because we bought them with our hard-earned cash and we shouldn't waste money. We fear that by getting rid of something that was part of a project we started, but never finished, we're admitting that we can't do something. We've let our possessions define us, so we fear that we will lose who we are when we get rid of them.

> "I used to be a ham radio operator. It was a big part of my life in high school and college. I've kept the equipment (and there is a lot of it) in my spare room for 20 years. I keep thinking I'll get back into it. One night, at a Clutterless meeting, I made a commitment to just look at it and figure out what was going on. I sat in the room all alone with my radios and paraphernalia. Memories flooded back to me of the good times I'd had using the stuff. I said good-bye to those memories, and actually cried. Then I envisioned the room as being empty and making it into a computer work-shop, something I love today. I sold the radio equipment on eBay and used to money to outfit the room for my current passion. I felt good about it, because the radio stuff went to someone who really wanted it and could use it. The fear behind my keeping it was that I'd be admitting I'd grown old and wasn't a college kid anymore. I'm not a college kid. I'm an adult with new toys. There just wasn't enough room for the new and the old toys. I made a choice. I never looked back."
>
> —C.B., clutterer

Decluttering and not-cluttering are about living in the now. We all had projects that gave us joy once. We all had projects that we never finished. That doesn't make us any less of a person. It makes us human. Facing our fears and doing something to combat them makes us self-actualized.

## This Is a Lifelong Commitment

You've probably read "how to organize" books, bought videos that promised to solve your cluttering forever, or seen people on Oprah who had a professional organizer (and, in one case, a team from 1-800-Got-Junk, a service that carts away stuff by the truckload) come in and transform their houses into clones of Martha Stewart's home. Guess what? Those quick-fixes do not work. They make good TV, but are bad humanity. No one is, or should be allowed to be, able to make the decisions for you about what is important and what is not. You are holding onto stuff for a reason, and, logical or not, it is your reason. If you let someone declutter and organize for you, you will still be living in the problem, not the solution. The clutter will come back in a few weeks or a few months and you will be in a troubled emotional state. Slow and sure wins the race.

If you're a clutterer, you'll probably always have cluttering tendencies. We can learn to understand our behavior, deal with the greater issues, and start living a relatively clutter-free life, but life is an up-and-down proposition. The only time it is flat is when we are dead. Just as an overeater can lose weight and change her eating habits by changing her relationship to food, a clutterer can change her relationship to things. But overeaters sometime revert back to previous behavior if they don't constantly monitor what's going on inside. Don't worry—this doesn't have to be an obsession or a narcissistic preoccupation. Just be aware that, when things don't go perfectly (and with kids what are the chances of that?), you'll sometimes clutter. So what? No one is perfect. We all have times when we do things we know we shouldn't. As we say at Clutterless meetings, "If I did it, I can undo it." Once you've changed your relationship to things to something that makes you happy, it is a lot easier to maintain a clutter-free life and to pick up after yourself when you have a cluttering episode.

The changes in your life will be subtle. The first step to living a clutterless life is to begin to appreciate space. This doesn't mean you need to start working for NASA. It is a fundamental change in our way of thinking. Right now, you value your possessions. You have a need to fill every available space with something. Otherwise, it looks bare, empty, and threatening. That's right, threatening. Here's a story from a clutterer who spent the night at a feng shui master's house:

> "I thought the experience would be a good one. After all, if I was to learn to appreciate space, then where better than in a house that had perfect feng shui? It was a very large house, tall enough for two stories, but it only had one, with high ceilings, creating a very airy feel. The furniture was minimalist. The bookcases were built into the wall, way up on rows around the ceiling, so you needed a ladder to get to them, rather like at a reference library. The bedroom had a

bed, no nightstand, and one table with a vase and a flower in it. At first, I felt clear in mind and spirit. But, when I tried to go to sleep I couldn't. I was uneasy. A terrible feeling overcame me. I felt like I was literally about to fly apart. There were not any boundaries. I felt lost. When I returned to the house of another friend who was neat, but had a more 'normal' house configuration, I felt far more comfortable."

Too tidy is too stressful. Clutterers need some things around them to feel comfortable. While this may appear to have some overtones of agoraphobia, I don't think we have that problem. We often have trouble defining ourselves and, to some extent, no matter how recovered we may become, we always will.

# Let's Get Practical

Theory is wonderful. It can help us understand what's going on, which is a first step towards change. But endless theorizing without action is a waste of time. You've got a problem because you like stuff too much. What can we do about it?

## Learn to Separate the Emotions From Things

Throwing clothes wherever and making messes of any kind aren't effective means of showing your anger with someone. The recipient of your anger doesn't care. The mess only makes *you* feel worse, thus giving those people even more power over your life. If you're depressed or anxious about something, don't let cluttering be your treatment of choice. When you clutter, you get more depressed about the mess and more anxious, because it ultimately means you won't be able to find things when you need them.

## Start Small

You didn't get this way overnight and you won't change in a weekend. Instead of a marathon decluttering session (unless you have your children's teacher or the in-laws coming, in which case, you have no choice), pick one area you will declutter and go to it. Make sure it is realistic. Clearing off a sofa, desk, or table (or even a few square feet of one) is realistic. Choose an area that has the least emotional attachment for you. Don't start with a closet full of clothes, not only because you want a visible area, but because clothes are often memory items for us. We hold onto dresses and suits that don't fit because we feel that someday we'll lose weight again and be able to wear them. Don't start with a pile of papers that contains bills and things you've been putting off because that requires a lot of decision-making. Decluttering a whole room is not realistic. Pick an area that's highly visible instead of a closet or drawer. This will show your family that you are trying.

One word of caution, though. Don't expect your family to congratulate you at first. While a Herculean task of cleaning off part of a sofa may seem like a huge accomplishment to you, your family is more likely to notice the rest of the house that is still cluttered. One of our life-changing goals is to get our appreciation from ourselves, not outside sources. At first, just setting a goal of decluttering for 15 minutes or working through an inch of debris may be all you can handle. Setting a goal of an hour is counterproductive. An hour can seem like an eternity. But 15 minutes seems short—perhaps too short. "If I did this for 15 minutes a day, my children will have grand-children before this place is livable." Not to worry. Usually, when we have completed a 15-minute segment, we feel so good about our progress that we add another 15 minutes, then another, and so on. Stop when you find your interest flagging or your resentment building up. With children in the house, it's unlikely that you'll have large blocks of time free anyway.

If you have little ones, choose your decluttering time during their naptime. If you have school-age children, either pick the time they're at school, if you don't work outside the home, or the time when they're sup-posed to be studying, if you have an outside job.

## Reward Yourself

Whenever you've made some small improvement, reward yourself. Take a bubble bath, go for a walk in the park, work on a woodworking project in the garage, get or make your favorite food, or do whatever makes you feel good. Oh dear, I have another caveat to give you: Don't go shopping!

## Once You've Gotten Started, Enlist Your Kids as Helpmates

It's best to make your first baby steps alone, so you can relish the feel-ing of your own success. That's why we started with something easy. Once that's done, you can make great strides in decluttering and get your kids to understand what it's all about for themselves, if you ask them to help. Pick obvious areas, which probably have a lot of their clutter too, where you can both see results quickly. Kids won't be able to help you with that pile of bills and papers underneath the ceramic turtle on your desk, but they can help in the common living areas.

Before you start, identify places where things live. The key is to make the places where they're going to put their own stuff easy to get to. What good are possessions if we can't possess them?

Make it a game. "Okay, kids, let's see what we can find in these piles of stuff. I bet you don't even know what's here!" Kids won't have as much trouble making decisions as you. They either like something or they don't. There'll be a few maybes, but not as many as you—the over-thinking adult—will have.

## Okay, Here Are a Few Common Clutter Pitfalls

This book isn't about rehashing all the decluttering tips you've read elsewhere, or even in my other books. The specifics about your kids' stuff will often apply to your own. Clutter is clutter. I've seen some books that are veritable encyclopedias of how to organize everything. Don't worry about that. Deal with the big issues, the psychological issues, and you'll do the "how to." I don't favor buying a lot of organizing knickknacks that just become more clutter. Your goal is to get rid of stuff, not to make it all nice and neat. Still, I've put together some of our more common addictions and some new ideas that you might stumble over in attaining your goals. They've all been clutter-tested by real clutterers.

### Newspapers and Magazines

If you have a tendency, like most clutterers, to enshrine newspapers, catalogs, and magazines, the kids can ease that burden on you. You save printed matter because they have articles you meant to clip or items you want to buy, or you feel like you should know everything. The kids don't have those concerns. Let them declutter your periodicals stash. They'll probably be big into recycling, so they'll feel good and see the larger purpose of not-cluttering by putting all those papers into the recycling bin. Oh, I know this may be hard for you. We clutterers feel we have to know everything, or that our job is to provide information for others. We don't and it's not. Trust me on this. Just this one time, let the kids recycle everything. When it comes to hugely emotionally laden items, it's not a good idea to let someone else do it, but newspapers and magazines are pretty low down on the emotionally significant scale. If there's something you really want to refer back to, it is most likely available on the Internet, and definitely at the library.

You want to clip articles to help others. That's a good trait, but when it gets in the way of living your life, it isn't so good. As much as you want to help others, is it really your responsibility? Isn't it possible that they've seen the same magazines or newspapers and can clip them for themselves if they want? Or are you trying to control their lives by "helping" them be more perfect? Information is out there in many different formats and people who need it will find it. Let them make their own discoveries. You aren't Magellan.

## Mail

This is a big clutter issue. Start backwards here. Set up a mailing center. Put a recycling basket by the mailbox or front door. Shredders eliminate the fear of someone rummaging through your trash and finding something. Plus, there's something rewarding about shredding clutter. You're showing it who's boss. Start with new mail first. Not letting any more pile up will be more effective than sorting through the old stuff, take less time, and be easier on you. Deal with it at the source. Just as your kids are more likely to put things away if you make it easy for them, so it is with adults. Junk mail (except for catalogs, which are a whole clutter subissue in themselves) can go into the recycle bin immediately. I know it's hard at first, but many clutterers can start here. They actually start to enjoy recycling or shredding and then recycling junk. It gives them a feeling of control about what comes into the house they are starting to be proud of. Open real mail at the mailbox and discard the envelope.

## Catalogs

Catalogs may be the hardest. They represent possibilities. There are so many pretty things in them that we'd like to have. However, if we didn't buy it six months ago, we probably aren't going to buy it today. You'll get a new catalog next month with the same items, if they're still available, or better ones. Prices from a catalog that is six months or a year old are hardly likely to be correct. If you try to eliminate the catalogs yourself, you'll waste countless hours thumbing through them and thinking "what if." Let the kids do it.

## Bills

How much money are you losing by forgetting to pay bills on time? Pay yourself the equivalent of the late charge when you pay them early. Write checks for bills as soon as they come in. If you have to wait for the money to get to the bank (What a concept—a clutterer with a balanced checkbook! Stranger things have happened.), then put the bill in a suspension file on the date you can safely mail it. Set up a chart of when they're due, either on a poster or on the computer. Give yourself a gold star for each one you pay on time.

## Recipes

Boy, oh boy, do we like recipes! I once shared a table at a booksellers event with a cookbook author. I complimented her on her book, and she said she hoped sales from this new one would be as good as her first one. I empathized, because I've published 17 books, and a couple of them seem to outsell the others. My book on living in Mexico, *Live Better South of the Border,* has been a perennial seller, with about 40,000 copies in print. I was pretty proud of that, until she told me her first cookbook sold a "mere" 240,000 copies. She did let me in on a little secret, though: People buy cookbooks, not necessarily because they are going to make all the recipes, but because of the *possibility* of preparing such wonderful dishes.

Nearly every clutterer I know has stacks of cookbooks and piles of recipes clipped from newspapers and magazines. One confessed at a Clutterless meeting, "I did an approximate inventory of the recipes I'd clipped. If I made one dish every day, I couldn't get through them if I lived another 110 years."

The key to discarding recipes is to accept our mortality. How long do you think you'll live? Long enough to go through them all? As a parent, how often are you able to cook elaborate or time-consuming meals for your family? Come on, be honest.

Let them go! Fly, little recipes, fly like the wind. Keep your recipe books if you must, because at least they're compact and neat. But folders of recipes from magazines and newspapers are messy. I know I'll get a lot of disagreement from die-hard recipe collectors, but most of those recipes are probably in books, perhaps with a few variations. If you must seek out new worlds where no cook has gone before, go online and join a recipe-swapping or cooking discussion forum. A Google search brought up "about 10,900" recipe sites, including *www.allrecipes.com, eat.epicurious.com,* and my favorite, *www.topsecretrecipes.com.* If you must feed your recipe addiction, please don't print them! Save them to a text file in a folder called, oh I don't know, "Recipes I'll never get to." If you feel the urge to be creative someday, you can browse through them on your word processor and pick the *one* you're going to try that day. Then pitch it. It'll always be there for you if you want to try it again. Talk about a constant lover!

## Knickknacks

Your kids will have laser-beam eyes when it comes to your extraneous paraphernalia. They'll see no value to that dusty gnome on your bookshelf. It may have been given to you by your dear Aunt Tillie and you're holding onto it just in case she ever comes to visit or as a memory of her. Make it a rule that, except for newspapers and the like, your kids have to ask you before discarding something. You'll learn a lot about yourself and your kids will learn that you are a human being as you try to justify some of the treasures you keep. The good news is that sometimes you won't remember why you're holding onto things and can let them go, because they've out-lived their usefulness. That's a good lesson for the kids to apply to their old toys, games, and clothes. The bad news is that you'll feel a pang of regret if you try to eliminate something that does have some sentimental attachment for you. Be easy on yourself. If a possession still means something to you, keep it. Your kids will learn from this too. Sentiment is a good thing. It's human. It will give them permission to keep some things just because they make them feel good.

## Plastic Bags and Boxes

I don't know a clutterer yet who's met a cardboard box she didn't like. Boxes are like recipes in a way. They represent potential. They could come in handy for storing things as we declutter. They could come in useful for packing those Christmas presents we're going to send 11 moths from now. Kids like boxes too, unfortunately. But at least they discriminate. Big boxes can become forts. Medium-sized boxes are good for storing stuff. Little boxes, except those that are already decorated, have no value.

"I have a 'box room.' It is supposed to be my sewing room, but little by little, it's been taken over by boxes. I know I'll never use them all, but I just can't get rid of them. They seem so useful. And you never know, I just might need one someday. The perfect box is in there somewhere."

—Tonisha,
a clutterer

Boxes are like relatives. They keep coming into our lives. Even though we seem to love boxes, few of us are really emotionally attached to them. Let your kids recycle them. Once you've regained the space the boxes used to steal from you, you might think twice the next time you get a darling box with something you buy. We keep the boxes our computers, monitors, scanners, small appliances come in, in case we have to ship them back to the manufacturer to be repaired. There's some logic to this, but not a lot. Keep the box (torn down) for the length of the return period (assuming you know where the receipt and warranty are!), then discard it.

## Breaking Your Box Fetish With Logic

I bought a cute little electronic waterfall for my bedroom. Naturally, I wanted to save the box in case I had to ship it back. Upon reading the warranty (which I also wanted to save), I discovered that I'd have to pay $9.95 to the company to fix it, plus shipping and insurance. The item cost me $12.95. Duh! The box and warranty went into the recycle bin. The fountain is still working two years later.

Most of the time, if something is defective, we take it back to the store where we bought it. Department stores claim they have to have the original packaging, but they'll take things back without it. Computer stores do not care about the boxes, they have plenty. It's a gamble, but the odds are on your side. Most things don't need to be returned, so we don't need to keep the boxes.

If you store the item in its box, the way I store my drill and electric saw in the boxes they came in, that's another story. If the box has a use, it's not clutter.

For the most part, your kids will be thrilled to recycle cardboard for you. In fact, of all the recycling we Americans do, cardboard is the only one that's really profitable. Did you know that most cardboard is shipped to Mexico, because they are the experts at recycling?

## Plastic Sacks

I know you have a box or cupboard full of plastic sacks from the grocery store. You keep meaning to drop them off in the convenient recycling box at the front of the store. But you just never get around to it. Those sacks multiply in the dark and will expand to take over your kitchen some day. Let the kids recycle them. Make it a habit that, when you get ready to go to the grocery store, the kids cart the plastic sacks to your car. If they go with you, they'll remember to take them inside. You probably won't. Following up on the Mexico recycling factoid above, Mexico's biggest litter problem is plastic sacks. When I started going there 30 years ago, plastic sacks didn't exist. Everyone carried their own shopping bags of burlap or plastic. There was very little litter. Such is the price of affluence. Come to think of it, you could apply this principle to your not-cluttering tactics. Bring your own permanent shopping bags to the grocery store and you won't have to deal with plastic sacks at all.

## Cottage Cheese Containers

These rank just below boxes in our hierarchy of potentially useful things. Maslow had his Hierarchy of Needs, and clutterers have theirs. They'd be great for storing leftovers. The deeper thing going on here is our fear of lack. We subconsciously fear (heck, how many of our fears are conscious?) that we'll never have enough, that we shouldn't waste things, so we keep those containers to alleviate two fears at once—rather a model of cluttering efficiency. Keep a few, because they really are good for storing food, but five are probably plenty (50 is more likely the number you've stashed). The kids might want one or two to store their paintbrushes or pens. Let them have them. Let the recycling bin gobble up the rest.

## Clothes

Your kids may be able to help you with these, but it's iffy. Most likely, they'll want to clean out your closet because everything you wear is so uncool. But it can be an important lesson for them to learn about decluttering their own closets. Cool is in the eye of the beholder. You should set some ground rules, both for your closet and theirs. First, pick out all the things that have obvious flaws such as stains that won't come out, rips, tears, buttons missing, zippers that don't work without a struggle, and so on. Put the stained items into one of those boxes you've stashed away for donation, if the stains aren't too bad. Even the poor have pride. I know lots of people who would have had nothing to wear if it weren't for donations, so remember that you're dealing with people, not a "class."

Before you start to separate the clothes that can be mended, ask yourself if you still like them. Then ask your kids if they ever remember you wearing it. If you get two nos, then why waste any more time on it. Donate it.

If you, or they, are handy with a needle and thread, then put the clothes that can be mended into a basket that's just for clothes that need to be fixed. If the basket starts to overflow, think about it. Do you have so many sewing projects lined up that you're like the recipe lady mentioned earlier? Good clothes that need mending are perfect for the donation box.

Oh, those good-looking clothes that just shrank! We all have them. It's not that we gained weight, they really did shrink in the night. And the memories they evoke! "I wore this when your Dad proposed." (Chances are that shrank several times.) "This is the maternity dress I wore when I was carrying you." (You might want to make sure you've already explained the birds and the bees if you bring this up, or you'll get sidetracked into an important but, for the moment, irrelevant conversation.) "This is the suit and tie I wore when I landed that dream job." (The chances of your kids appreciating any tie are slim, so take their comments in this area with a couple of grains of salt.)

You're going to hold onto some memory clothes. We all do. Your kids, however, will prove a reality check. And, sneaky you, you're teaching them a lesson about their own memory clothes. When the time comes to clean out their closet and they just can't get rid of 90 percent of the things in there, you'll be able to refer back to the time they helped you decide what to keep and what to toss.

Space in your closet is really the final frontier. It's hard to get rid of clothes. If we create some space for the things we cherish, we give them respect. We don't crush everything together. And we can find them when we want to wear them.

## Clothes That Belonged to Someone Who's No Longer in Your Life

If you're dealing with the clothes of a deceased loved one, this could be a great time for both you and your children to savor some memories and say good-bye. As I said elsewhere, don't do this until you are ready, not when some well-meaning friend or relative thinks you should do it. Your kids might surprise you here. They'll have memories of your partner that you didn't even think they had. There'll most likely be more than a few tears shed during this exercise, so set aside a big block of time when you can be alone with your children and you don't have other challenges you're dealing with. This will be the hardest and most fulfilling decluttering you can ever do.

We don't want to discard these items. We feel that we are discarding the person. We aren't. Those we love are with us always, in our hearts, not our closets. Your children may feel this even more than you. Chances are, they already have items given to them by the deceased. They may want one or two things in the closet. Let them have them. They aren't ready to say good-bye yet.

You've got two choices here: You can save most of the items in a box in the attic, so you won't have to face the emotion of "discarding them," or you can ask yourself if your beloved would rather you donate them to someone who can use them. Gucci dresses and Oscar de la Renta suits could help some strangers advance in their careers and create a better life for their children. So could off-the-rack items from Sears. You could sell them to a resale shop if money is tight. Or you could do nothing, close the closet door and leave them be. It's up to you. Whatever you do will be right for you. Whatever you do will be a valuable lesson for your children. They will learn that adults have feelings too, and that love knows no boundaries of space or time. When we really love, we love forever. We've all lost people in our lives, and your children will lose people from their lives. Learning that death is part of life now may aid them in dealing with the deaths that are sure to come as they grow older. Whatever you do, do it with gentleness and ceremony. Your kids will always remember.

## Irrational Fears

This is the root of all the other emotions that cause a clutterer to avoid throwing things out. Clutterers are afraid of making a mistake. They fear that if they throw out something, they'll discover they needed it after all. The main reason we stay disorganized has nothing to do with "systems." It has to do with our fears. Some of our fears are:

- Fear of making a mistake.
- Fear of not doing something perfectly.
- Fear of failure, so we don't upset the status quo.
- Fear of making a decision.
- Fear of throwing out the one thing that we need.

This is a frequent topic at Clutterless meetings. You can do this at home. Imagine a time when you *did* throw out something you felt you needed later. Then remember the consequences of not having it. How great were they? Everyone agreed that, at the time, the consequences seemed terribly important. But, with the passage of time, they really were insignificant. If the facts or ideas were really valuable, they were probably available somewhere else.

We can take the knowledge of having discarded something and the world not having come to an end and apply that to the next time fear tries to stop us from decluttering. We did it once and the consequences were not as great as we feared. We can do it again.

With that self-knowledge, we're better prepared to sort through that stack of papers or files and make decisions about the relative value of them. We may still hold onto a fair number of them, but we'll be able to let go of more than we thought. Try it. Make yourself a safety net. Put those things you think *might* be valuable into a box. After a month or two, note how many of them you have retrieved. This will make it easier the next time to be more decisive.

# Control

I do not believe that we cannot control our clutter. In fact, I unequivocally state that we can turn that misplaced control issue to our advantage. As in judo, we use our opponent's force to our advantage. We learn to control the things in our lives instead of using things to control the people in our lives.

That, my friends, is what this book and the clutterless philosophy is all about. We learn to place people first in our lives and things second. We learn to take back our lives.

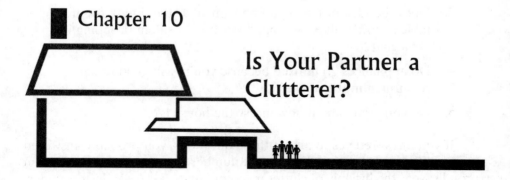

# Chapter 10

# Is Your Partner a Clutterer?

*Our marriage was in trouble. I'd just given up on getting Linda to ever get organized. I could live with the empty boxes in the garage, but the hundreds of cottage cheese containers, the newspapers piled up everywhere, and the piles of papers on the stairs were overwhelming. More kept coming in and nothing ever went out. Once we both started attending Clutterless Recovery Group meetings, our lives changed. We are both more content and I understand why it's so hard for her. It wouldn't be too strong to say that the meetings have saved our marriage.*

—Sam, a non-cluttering spouse

*As clutter relates to families, I cannot tell you how many people I have met whose marriages are threatened by clutter.*

—Jan Jasper, professional organizer

Quick! What's the difference between your house and a storage shed? If you can't answer that without thinking, then you're either a clutterer yourself or are patient enough to still be partners with one. Trust me, you aren't alone. Here's a short quiz based on common conditions at clutterers' houses:

1. Are you ashamed to have friends and family over?

2. Are your kids ashamed to invite their friends over?

3. Does the idea of having a family meal at the dining-room table sound as likely to happen as the President dropping in for a chat?

4. Do appliances go unfixed because you're ashamed to have repairmen in the house?

5. Do you argue about how messy the house is?

If you answered yes to any of these questions, you probably answered yes to all but number four. If you got number four "right," then you can proudly wear the insignia of clutterer spouse, first-class (oak clusters underneath a stack of boxes) on your sleeve. You earned it.

If you're the neat one, my sympathies go out to you. Living with a clutterer is quite a challenge. Some spouses cope with it by just giving up and accepting that their houses will always be a mess. Others nag. More have stopped saying anything, but walk around their partner on eggshells, afraid to say anything about the elephant in the living room (in most cases this is a figure of speech, though clutterers often have an abundance of cats), full of pent-up anger. The good news is that there are solutions, and understanding is the key.

## You're Going to Gain a Lot More Than a Clean House

If your clutterer is willing to do the emotional and psychological work necessary to change their cluttering behaviors, you'll both benefit on many levels. But, as I've said before, the clutterer has to want to change and then be willing to work on emotional and psychological issues. Your job is to encourage and support—not to do. That's the clutterer's job. The dynamics of your relationship will change. Control issues you didn't even know you had will change. A lot of tension will dissipate. If you can work together as a team, you can rebuild a marriage that has had a third, disruptive partner. It'll be hard for you to "do nothing," as you may view it. But, trust me, I've seen the rewards from applying the principles you're about to learn pay off in ways you cannot now imagine.

## If You're Both Clutterers

If you're both clutterers, get two copies of this book, because one of you will misplace it. The natural tendency in a double-clutterer family is to think, *"I could get organized if he or she would just get his or her clutter out of my way."* (From now on, I'm going to alternate the pronouns "he" and "she." Both men and women can be clutterers.) My Website surveys and attendance at Clutterless Recovery Groups (*www.clutterless.org*) have shown that about 65 percent of those who seek help for cluttering are women. On the other hand (there's always another hand, except when it comes to cleaning up), a psychiatrist friend of mine told me not to read too much into that. Women are more likely than men to admit they have a problem and then to do something about it.

## The Effect on Kids

"Did I have friends over? Not many. I was always really careful about who I would invite over or let come in. Some made mean comments. I was never really comfortable. Their body language made it apparent that they weren't really comfortable."

—Enrique, son of a clutterer

"There was always a lot of tension in the house. Dad hated the clutter. Sometimes they'd fight about it. I wished I'd lived with more normal parents. The funny thing is, I ended up like my mom—cluttered. I feel clutter has cost me relationships. I try to keep my boyfriends from coming to my apartment. When they see the way I live, they go away. I could never seem to sustain a neat apartment. It just seems so natural to come in and just drop things everywhere, leave dishes in the sink, and so on. I feel ashamed, but I still don't change. I feel like I can never live with anyone unless I change. I feel like there's something really wrong with me that can't be fixed."

—Michelle, daughter of a clutterer

Whether your kids identify with the clutterer or the non-cluttered partner, they know what's going on. If clutter's causing tension in your relationship, it's causing them stress. They'll see the battle going on between their parents and may feel like they have to choose sides. Just like all the positive things you've tried to teach them, they're learning the negative ones too. Parents change a lot of their behaviors for their children. Changing this one certainly isn't easy, but it can certainly be done.

# What Doesn't Work

- Traditional organizing methods.
- Nagging.
- Just giving up.
- Praying silently (without taking appropriate action).
- "Helping" your spouse clean up.
- Referring to your clutterer with negative words such as *messie, pack rat, clutterbug, slob.*
- Sanitizing the condition by calling it collecting, or overstating it by calling it hoarding.

## Traditional Organizing Methods

Your spouse has probably tried traditional organizing methods. How do I know? Years of experience and working with thousands of clutterers has taught me that this is the first thing people try. Organizing methods help, but only temporarily, until the clutterer changes the underlying cluttering behavior. Without even coming to your house (as if you'd open the door!) I can tell you what happened. The tips and tricks worked for a few weeks or maybe even a month or two. After that, things got back to normal—cluttered.

The previous list isn't meant to make anyone feel guilty or feel like a failure. You've done the best you could with what you knew. You've probably seen "organizing experts" on TV or read articles in popular magazines and books on organizing. These all made perfect sense to you. Just formulate a plan, create a space for everything, and follow the plan. Gosh, how simple is that? It's simple to the people who develop these approaches because they aren't clutterers.

## Organizing the Stuff Works—For Others
## and for Clutterers Who've Dealt With the Real Issues

There's nothing wrong with traditional organizing methods. They work—for people who just need some direction and instructions on how to organize. And they can work for clutterers, once the clutterer is ready to change the underlying behavior. Until then, they're a source of frustration for both parties and a waste of time. They may actually make the situation worse. Clutterers are pretty smart people. The rules of organizing are logical and simple. It should be easy for a smart person to follow them. When they can't, they get frustrated. The whole exercise becomes yet one more example of their failure in this area of their life. They give up on themselves and look at any further organizing tips as criticism. It's like when a kid gets criticized so often that he shuts down and hears only criticism, even when none is intended.

At a Clutterless meeting, one woman proclaimed tearfully, "I'm a smart woman. Why can't I just follow the rules in those organizing books?"

The answer is that they weren't written for us or by us. My books are.

## But I Bought Her the Best-Selling Books on Organizing!

I understand. It's not like you haven't tried. You've given the cluttered half of your team books and clipped magazine articles to help her. You thought you were doing the right thing. After all, the author was a recognized "expert" and had been interviewed on *Oprah* or in *USA Today* or some such national outlet. She'd published articles in national magazines and ran a successful organizing business. People want sound, simple solutions to serious lifelong problems. Let's try real, life-changing solutions now.

The authors of organizing books are sincere in their belief that their books help people. Organizing books, for the most part, are written by organized people for normal people who are not emotionally entangled in their spiderwebs of stuff. Some books have made attempts to address the emotional component, but to me and the clutterers I've talked to, those books fell short of understanding us.

One popular author even admits she was a "slob," but decided to change. Good for her, though it's sad that she used that negative stereotype. Some people can just decide to change. I know alcoholics who just decided to change and did. Most, however, realize that they need to change more than their drinking habits to live a happy life. They need to change their thinking habits. They choose to go to AA meetings. So it is with clutterers. They need to change the mentality that makes them hold onto stuff. It's a lifelong process, and a support group is the best solution.

Non-clutterers (people who are sometimes a little messy) are able to take some direction about how to organize and how to determine if something is worth keeping without too much difficulty. Clutterers are the greatest consumers of "how to get organized" books. We'll clutch at any straw to keep ourselves from drowning in our own clutter.

You may even have bought this book, hoping that just one more book would turn the tide. This time you were right. This book could start a real change, particularly if coupled with my first book on cluttering, *Stop Clutter From Stealing Your Life*. But books alone won't help as much as if your clutterer joins a support group.

### Professional Organizers Do What They Do Well

Professional organizers are fine, caring people who are good at what they do. Their skills are useful to their clients. A few have even confided to me that they're clutterers at home. It's easier for anyone to organize someone else. Those who work most effectively with clutterers understand that we need to sever the emotional ties to our things before we can start applying organizing principles. Most organizers will admit that working with a real clutterer is a big challenge. This is because they concentrate on the stuff (and rightly so, because they aren't counselors). The stuff is only part of the problem. It's how your clutterer relates to the stuff that needs to change first. Those clothes choking their closets aren't just pieces of cloth. They are memories.

## Nagging

I know how frustrating it is to live with a clutterer. I've been on both sides of that equation. It's like being in a foreign country, where, out of frustration, some people just repeat their desires in a louder voice. We know that it won't make our language any more intelligible to a Frenchman, but we just don't know what else to do.

In a way, the clutterer speaks a foreign language. It makes perfect sense to you to say, "Why can't you just throw the newspaper out when you're done with it?" To the clutterer, there are two foreign concepts in the preceding sentence—"throw out" and "done with it." Most clutterers understand what a newspaper is.

Clutterers never throw anything out. They have to recycle. They have to give it to just the right person. They have to be good stewards of everything that comes into their lives. Clutterers are never "done with" something. They have to apply these principles to everything. Information has to be absorbed, finally read (that's why they're saving magazines and newspapers), reread, passed on to someone who needs it, clipped, filed, and saved. Broken items have to be put somewhere so they can be mended—someday. Clothes have to be stored until they magically fit again or can be given to just the right person.

While nagging may work for the short term, with both adults and your kids, this "solution" is worse than the problem. One of the reasons for cluttering is rebellion. Nag someone, and they might do what you want, just to get you off their back for the present, but they'll find a way to "show you" later. There's a better way.

## Just Giving Up

This is like reverse nagging. Giving up and pretending you don't care may seem like the answer. It keeps peace in the family. You may mask your reaction by calling it acceptance. It's more like enabling. I'm a big believer in accepting the things we can't change (like other people), but I like to be honest about knowing the difference between what I can and can't change. If you're living in a messy home and hate it, your feelings are going to come out, somehow, someway. We can repress our feelings, but we can't deny them. (You might like the Shadow Self discussion in Chapter 9.) When we give up hope that things will change, we ensure they won't.

## Praying Silently (Without Taking Appropriate Action)

I'm a big fan of prayer. So are most people. But it doesn't do any good to pray for a pony unless you take the actions necessary to obtain a pony. You've already taken the first step—you're reading this book, trying to understand what to do. Give a little prayer of thankfulness right now for this book having come into your life. Here are the tools to answer your prayers. You're going to get that pony after all!

## "Helping" Your Spouse Clean Up

Please do *not* use the phrase, "Give me a weekend and a shovel and I'll get rid of all your clutter."

"I have a tendency to hoard things. I experience a high level of stress when faced with even the prospect of parting with my stuff. This feeling of acute anxiety could be related to an experience I had when I was 11 or so. I discovered that my mom had thrown away all of my past artwork. I was overcome with a sense of sadness and grief. I felt vulnerable and naked, stripped of my identity, and shorn of any resource I had in which to witness the evolution of myself as an artist.

"What made matters worse was that my mom was unrepentant. She said that our recent move out of our former house had prompted her to get rid of a lot of "nonessentials" and that this was a healthy thing to do. She said that she had thrown my art away along with a lot of other physical possessions. She went on to explain that these things were just things and that we shouldn't live life burdened by our belongings."

—Maria, a recovering clutterer

You may have seen TV shows where a family member "cleans up" or "organizes" someone's house without their consent. That's one of the cruelest things you can do to anyone. What you haven't seen is the emotional trauma and even nervous collapses that "clutter cure" causes after the TV cameras are gone. I have too many stories from clutterers who've had that done to them. It caused a permanent rift in their relationships. They felt violated, discarded, and abused. They lost all trust for the relative who did it to them.

I know you want to help and you're acting out of love (okay, maybe with a little, teeny-weeny bit of frustration too). You know the value of things. If your partner's difficulty is making decisions about what's valuable and what's not, then why not do a Mars/Venus mind meld and help her get rid of the junk? Wrong, Mr. Spock. You're applying logic to an illogical situation. You don't have enough data. You want to jump in, like a commando behind enemy lines, identify the enemy's positions, and call in an air strike.

Maybe you feel your spouse just needs a little nudge to get started (yeah, I know I said that procrastination is a clutterer's trait, but bear with me). There's a big difference between a nudge and a push.

### How Can You Really Help?

Remember how we talked earlier about rewarding your children for making small strides in cluttering and learning how to not-clutter? Rewards work well with adults too, though it may have to be a trip to a *Chez Pompous* instead of McDonalds. Smiles, hugs, kisses, and positive comments are cheaper and work just as well.

First, accept that decluttering and learning to live an uncluttered life will take your partner some time. There will be many small steps, a few huge jumps in improvement, and some setbacks along the way. When you start getting frustrated at his progress, try to remember that any progress is better than what you've been living with. I've seen clutterers stumble along, making baby steps of improvement, and then, all of a sudden, a lightbulb goes on in their heads. They declutter more in a few days than they had for months before. Have faith and don't give up.

## A Success Story

"I was thrilled when Yolanda started going to Clutterless meetings. She came home in so much more of a positive mood that it would have been worthwhile for just that. But when she told me her commitment to the group was to clear off an inch of our dining-room table, I was dubious. At that rate, we'd be collecting Social Security before we had a livable house. But complaining about the mess hadn't worked, so I held my tongue. Sure enough, she did her inch. Then she was so excited about that she cleared off about a foot. I congratulated her for her achievement, even though I thought to myself, 'I could have cleared the whole table and then some in less time.'

"The next week, she actually made enough space for one person to eat. Up until then, we'd been balancing our plates on piles of stuff. I tried not to get my hopes up, because we had cleared it all off one time when we had company coming over and it was back to being a mess in a few weeks. But this time she said something about learning to make decluttered spaces 'sacred,' and she kept each area clear. Well, it's been nearly a year now, and we have enough clear space in the house that it's actually livable. I've learned by watching her how painful it is to do this stuff, and sometimes I just give her a little hug to let her know I appreciate her efforts. Our house wouldn't make the cover of *House Beautiful*, but it's certainly more peaceful. That's the greatest gift of all.

"The kids seemed to pick up on the changes and have been picking up things they used to leave lying around. I am cautiously optimistic that our lives will continue to improve."

—Enrique,
husband of a clutterer

## Referring to Your Clutterer With Negative Words

Cluttering is cluttering. Calling it something else trivializes it, encourages the clutterer's negative self-image, hurts his feelings, or overstates the seriousness of the condition. *Messie, clutterbug, pack rat,* and the like, sound cute, but they are designed to make one smile about something that's not very serious. Cluttering is serious. Clutterers know how it has limited their lives and self-esteem. People who use terms such as these are as aware of the real issue as those who say that alcoholics "get a little tipsy" or "just can't handle their liquor." Calling a clutterer a slob is like a slap in the face. A slob is someone who makes a mess and doesn't care. Clutterers care. They would rather not be the way they are, they just don't know how to change.

## Sanitizing or Overstating the Condition

Instead of demeaning our clutterer, we may try to call their cluttering by a less offensive term. Some people believe that, by using the term "collectors," they can defuse the stigma of being a clutterer. A collector is someone who has an identifiable collection of related items. He can find them, when he desires to look at them, and has arranged them in an understandable manner. A clutterer may collect related items (dolls, statues, plates, and so on), but they are jumbled. The clutterer will continually purchase more of these, but not store them in any recognizable fashion. A collection is clutter when it is just a jumble. Collectors know what they have and display their collections for their own enjoyment or that of others. Call something by its name and you own it. Call it something else and you hide from it.

Can a clutterer become a collector? Absolutely! In fact, one of the benefits of changing our cluttering habits is to take pride in those things that we own and care about. When a clutterer changes her habits, she will eliminate that which is not important and proudly cherish those things that have value. So don't ask a clutterer to throw out a collection that has meaning, but help her to enjoy her collection.

Hoarding is a very serious psychological condition affecting a very small percentage of people—less than 1 percent of the population. Hoarders keep garbage. Clutterers don't. Other hoarders keep large numbers of animals, usually cats and dogs, and make the news when the health department is called in. We frequently read stories in the press about people who live in houses stuffed to the rafters with old newspapers, boxes, and who knows what else. The most famous case of hoarding was that of the Collyer brothers, Homer and Langley, of New York, who made quite a splash in the 1942 newspapers. They had secluded themselves from the outside world and filled their mansion with several tons of clutter, including old newspapers, a grand piano, and indescribable trash. Homer was blind and housebound, so he depended on Langley to bring him food. He died of starvation after Langley was crushed in a collapse of newspapers and debris, crawling though the tunnels that were the only means of navigating the house.

# What Does Work

- Understanding the emotions behind cluttering.
- Acceptance.
- Willingness to change.
- Taking baby steps.
- Making decluttering a family affair.

## Understanding the Emotions Behind Cluttering

Understanding what's going on and making excuses are not the same thing. It doesn't take years of therapy to understand why clutterers keep things. Identifying the emotional attachment is only the first step. Once your clutterer realizes that she's holding onto things for invalid reasons, her job is to face those reasons and then take action.

Your partner clutters for reasons that aren't clear to him. He may keep clothing because he doesn't want to admit defeat in his weight control program. She may keep innumerable baby items because she's afraid to lose her baby. The child may grow up, but the baby who held or wore those items will always be there if she doesn't discard them. For some, the discarding of items used or worn by others is tantamount to discarding the person. He may keep old newspapers, catalogs, and magazines for fear of not knowing something he feels he should know, closing the door on opportunities, or out of a desire to be helpful and clip information and send it to someone who could use it.

There are a lot more emotions that come into play, and it took me two complete books to cover most of them. What's important here is to understand that people keep clutter in their lives for illogical reasons. Once you understand that, you're better able to help the clutterer in your family.

If you can listen to her feelings about stuff with an open mind and not interrupt or offer advice or opinions, then discuss it together. That's highly unlikely, unless you're a saint. One of the values of a support group is that clutterers can talk about how they feel when they try to declutter without comment or criticism. They do get a lot of nods of understanding, however. If there's no support group in your area, encourage her to find a nonjudgmental friend with whom she can share her feelings about cluttering. It will do a world of good for both of you.

### Fear of Being Criticized

Fears are at the root of the emotions that keep a clutterer from throwing things out. The fears are listed in Chapter 9, but there's another fear that applies here. Clutterers are afraid of making a mistake. Worse, they've probably learned that they'll get criticized for the wrong things they do and not noticed for the right ones. Given that scenario, what would you do? *Nothing* is the right answer.

We're perfectionists. (I know, your mind just added "perfect slobs." Old habits are hard to break.) One of the reasons we don't finish things or don't do them in the first place is a fear that we'll do them imperfectly or make a mistake. So our "solution" is to do nothing, or do one insignificant project perfectly, ignoring the bigger picture.

You can help by letting the clutterer make her own mistakes, just as you let your children make theirs, in order to learn from them. Then be there for her. Don't criticize her mistakes, but give her strokes for what she does right. Believe me, the clutterer is so good at self-criticism that she doesn't need any help from you to feel bad.

## *You Can't Do the Decluttering for Another Person, but You Can Support Her*

The clutterer has to do the work for herself. It does help to have a fellow clutterer to be a buddy, but it's hard for a non-cluttering partner to help without sounding judgmental. In a way, it's like letting your children help you with a project. You could get it done a lot faster if you just did it yourself, but it's the process that's important. If she wants, you can just be there for moral support. The kids can be great buddies, and they can work on their own clutter at the same time, or help Mom or Dad.

## Acceptance

I've worked with a lot of families who've told me that the greatest thing about attending clutterless support meetings is that the non-clutterer learns to apply acceptance to their lives. This doesn't mean giving up or accepting that your house will always be a cluttered mess. It does mean that, once you accept that your clutterer is not doing the odd things he does on purpose or to upset you, you'll cease taking it personally. When you accept that he is truly trying to change and that it is a long and difficult process, you will experience more peace in your home life. Little by little, your house will get to a degree of neatness that you desire, and you will learn to accept that it will never be perfect. But it will be a home where the two of you have reached a compromise.

## Willingness to Change

In order for any behavioral modification to work, there has to be an awareness that something is not the way you want it to be, and then you need to be willing to make the changes in your habits so that you can experience growth. Let's face it, clutterers *like* some of the results of their cluttering. They feel comfortable living in clutter. They're afraid to make the changes, because clutter has been their friend for years, much the same as an alcoholic fears stopping drinking, because he knows only that way of life. Once he believes that a new way of life has more to offer than the old life, he can change. It's the same with clutterers. They become willing to change, and they make the changes. The most frustrating thing for a spouse is the seeming unwillingness of their cluttering partner to do anything about it. A lot of that is tied to fears and emotional issues already discussed. When you take the steps outlined and make your relationship one of battling this condition together, the clutterer will feel less threatened and become willing to change the old behaviors. They won't change all at once, but, slowly, they will.

## Taking Baby Steps

Your clutterer isn't going to change overnight, nor will an entire cluttered room morph into Tidyville in one day or one week. It's best to set concrete goals in one area that's the most bothersome or obvious. As in the earlier story of Yolanda and Enrique, deciding to do an inch of a table or to work on something for 15 minutes works well. What usually happens is that when the clutterer achieves some success, she keeps going. Some, like me, become like the Energizer Bunny and keep going and going and going. Marathon sessions aren't best for everyone, but for some people they work. The drawback is that they tire a person out so much that they won't want to do any decluttering for a few days afterwards. The challenge is to keep a large area that was just decluttered "sacred," which means that nothing goes there except what belongs.

### Sacred Spaces Are the Key to Maintaining a Decluttered Lifestyle

Most clutterers have had "clean up" or "get organized" marathons that didn't have any lasting results. The real key is to declare an area sacred. For example, only dishes and meals go back onto the dining-room table. Mail doesn't. Newspapers don't. They go to other specific areas. What happens is a mental, behavioral change. The clutterer incorporates a mental habit of checking before putting something down. She catches herself putting something inappropriate on the table, for instance. You can help, in a gentle way, just by asking "sacred?" when you see her forgetting.

## Make Decluttering a Family Affair

"I decided that the couch would be a good project to help my family live a more normal life. Most people we know use their couches to sit on, not to dump junk on. The whole thing was too much to tackle, so I divided it up into North, South, East, and West. Each week, I worked on one compass point. It was a huge project because there were piles of stuff several feet high. The little ones helped, because they weren't attached to the stuff and had fun carrying old newspapers to the recycle bin as I let go of them. My husband, who is a dear, would come up and give me a gentle hug unexpectedly. He knew better than to try and help.

"As we got one cushion cleared, my family started a tradition of a 'clutter dance.' It was simple, really, but everyone joined hands and danced around in whatever clear area they could find. They'd sing, 'Clutter gone, clutter gone.' The little ones loved it. 'Mommy, when can we do a clutter dance?' they'd ask.

"It took several weeks, but finally we could all sit on the couch. We hadn't sat on that couch for years. Then I worked on the coffee table, and eventually, we could actually do a clutter dance around it. What a day! I felt so proud and my husband and kids told me how proud they were of me. To this day (a year later), while our house is not clutterless, that couch and table are still usable."

—Margot,
a very reformed clutterer

Involving the family in the decluttering projects helps everyone. If the kids are cluttered, they can work on their own clutter in the family area. Decluttering alone is hard. Having someone else there makes it easier. Aw heck, I wish I could say it was fun, but I'd be fibbing. However, if you have some kind of family ritual to follow successful decluttering, that part can be the "carrot" reward to replace the "stick" of nagging.

## Control Issues

Remember that I said control was a big factor in your kids' cluttering behavior? It's the same with adults. When a clutterer gets rid of his clutter, he fears he's losing control. It's like an alcoholic who quits drinking. Because of his previous behavior, he was able to control the family. Booze was his best friend. Take the booze away and he is bereft. In some families, the nondrinker controls the family. Control is a complicated and not always obvious issue. You may find that you were able to control your cluttering partner because of her lower self-esteem and guilt. When the first gets higher and the second dissipates, as she learns to control her own life, you may find that a new sense of independence will emerge. Because this will be a gradual change, you can both talk about it and learn to deal with it on your own terms. If you can't, it couldn't hurt to seek professional counseling. Clutter could have been masking a control issue in your family.

Ideally, the clutterer will give or throw away a lot of stuff. Realistically, she'll get rid of a lot, but still keep more than you think she should. Be patient. She's letting go of a way of life. Encourage your clutterer to decide where things go. Try to keep her focused, guiding without directing, as decluttering could degenerate into a redecorating project. We all know how long that can drag out.

Within the parameters of the space you have, let her decide where stuff goes that she absolutely can't get rid of. As Archie Bunker used to say, "Stifle yourself," when you're tempted to mention the irrationality of holding onto, say, those old clothes she's "going to mend one day." We both know that day will probably never come, but so what? When she's ready to let them go, they will go. I know, just moving things from one part of the house to another or to the garage doesn't seem like progress, but it's a start. The really important thing is that she make the newly decluttered areas sacred, so new clutter doesn't take the place of former clutter.

# In Conclusion

I sincerely believe that love and understanding really do conquer all. Clutterers sometimes hold onto their stuff to fill empty spots in their hearts. This could be from a fear of never having enough or a fear of not being loved. It could date back to their childhood or a time before they met you. Don't take it personally. But do take it as an opportunity to do what you can to make your relationship more important than things. If your clutterer doesn't seem ready to work on the problem, you may have to choose what's more important—the relationship or having a neat house.

Any clutterer who wants to change needs some motivation. Refer your cluttering partner to the Appendix of this book for the promises of what a not-cluttering life can bring.

Some partners have been satisfied if they have their own space. If you can have a spare room that's just yours, claim it. Clutterers will generally respect that it's off-limits. If you don't have that much free space, agree that a quarter or half of a room is yours. We all need our space and clutterers tend to take over. Firmness in maintaining your own space isn't being unkind—it's necessary for your own sanity. If you don't have a sanctuary, your frustration will seethe within you and, one day, boil over. Pressure cookers have an escape valve to keep the lid from blowing off. Find your pressure-release valve.

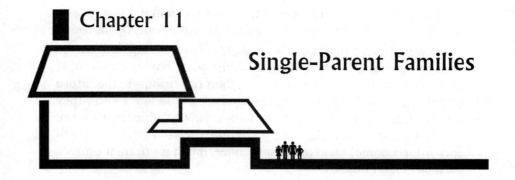

# Chapter 11

# Single-Parent Families

*Being a parent is a tough job, no matter how you look at it, and being a single parent makes that job that much tougher.*

—Dr. Benjamin Spock

Whatever your beliefs about single parenting, the reality is that roughly half of today's kids do grow up in single-parent households. This book would be incomplete if it didn't address the special issues these families face regarding cluttering and their children's relationship to stuff. In many ways, children's relationships to material possessions and emotional transference are more complicated in single-parent homes.

Single-parent families have special challenges (and some benefits) in relation to cluttering and children. While the stress of living in a single-parent family can contribute to cluttering behavior, at least there is only one adult to establish the neatness index of a household. In the long run, love is the most important possession you have to give.

Here's an observation by a wonderful mother who's found balance between cluttering, raising a family alone, and what's truly important:

"I am a widow with three wonderful, active boys. Two of them are clutter boys, mainly because they do not have their own rooms, but will help if asked or bribed. The third child is not a clutter boy and maintains his own room. He also takes out the trash, runs errands and does laundry once in a while. However, he works for Hollywood Video and attends classes to become a Dental Assistant and therefore is too busy to help very often with clutter outside his room.

"I was always a dedicated housekeeper before I married, maybe even too perfect, but have had to adjust since having children. If my two clutter boys hopefully receive their own rooms in the future I think they will do better. The youngest is now 13 and I know they will all depart someday soon, so I have simply adjusted to more clutter because when they are gone and I have a perfectly clean and orderly home, I will miss them more, much more than I miss a perfectly clean house now."

—Laura Martin Buhler, a.k.a. "The Gentle
Survivalist," *http://www.infowest.com/gentle*

## Being a Single Parent Doesn't Mean You Can't Be a Good Parent

So often, single parents fear that they won't be able to do as good a job as a two-parent household. In a perfect world, no one would die prematurely and no one would get divorced. Every kid would grow up with two loving parents. *Loving* is the operative word here. Whether kids are in two-parent or one-parent households, love and respect are the most important ingredients.

Dr. Michael Bradley, author of *Yes, Your Teen Is Crazy!* and *Yes, Your Parents Are Crazy*, said this in an interview about the efficacy of being a single parent:

> "It boils out to the nature of the child and the parent. A single parent can do just as good a job as two parents. Single parents who have maintained a loving relationship with their child may do better because the children do mature a little more. Single parents who complain about their divorce have more problems. That kid comes to love and respect the mother when she is not complaining."

Single parents face special challenges with their kids regarding cluttering. They may let their kids get away with cluttering, because they're afraid of losing their love by setting down too many rules. Don't fall into this trap. Rules define relationships. Kids won't love you any less for establishing rules. It takes off their burden of trying to figure out what's expected.

## When Things Are More Than Things

Your child may live with the other parent, but keep stuff at your house that seems like clutter to you. Kids keep things for reasons, and aren't always aware of those reasons. The following story, from Angie, a single mother, shows how "memory items" are just as important as the everyday things they keep at your house:

> "My daughter lives in California with her dad. He makes more money than I do, and can offer her more, so it made sense to let her stay there. He's not a bad person, but he works all the time. His new wife has done a great job of relating to Lilly. I wanted to clear out Lilly's room at my home and called to tell her. I told her that her room will always be there for her when she comes to visit, but it was just too full of stuff. She was willing to let go of a lot of 'kid things,' but there was one stumbling block.
>
> "'Mom, whatever you do, don't throw away those dresses Dad bought me when I was a little girl.'
>
> "'But honey, you're a teenager now. They don't even fit you.'
>
> "'I don't care. Throw them out and I won't come to visit.'
>
> "Teens seem to have a sixth sense about ways to hurt with words. I did feel frightened and hurt, but then I started to think about it. She loves her dad, and me, too. Keeping those things that her dad had given her at my home is her way of maintaining the relationship. It's like those clothes represent a physical contact with her father. The last thing I wanted to do was sever those ties. Who knows, there may be some things I gave her when she was a young child that she keeps at the other house. Things can be an important tie to people. The dresses are still in her closet when she comes to visit. We never mentioned the incident again."

## Different Houses, Different Rules

> "Essential in any parenting partnership is each parent's right
> to a personal parenting style. What Mom does at her house
> is her business. You may disagree with the other's lack of
> structure, rules about TV or homework, eating habits,
> bedtime or sleeping arrangements, but you no longer have
> the right to criticize the other parent's choices. As long as
> no harm is being done to your children...the other parent
> can relate to the children as he or she sees fit."
>
> —Stephanie Marston
> (*www.stephaniemarston.com*),
> author of *The Divorced Parent*

I highly recommend Stephanie Marston's book *The Divorced Parent*. It is practical and written from the heart. The above quote was followed by a story of a cluttering dad, a neat mother, and the challenges of dealing with that.

Attitudes about children's cluttering and possessions may be complete opposites in the two households. You didn't change the other parent while you were together, and you won't change him now. Take the Beatles' advice and let it be. Your kids won't be damaged by being exposed to different neatness styles. Ultimately, they'll choose which one appeals to them.

## More Stuff

Even if the part-time parent isn't a clutterer, he may try to buy the children's affection by being more lenient, or just plain buying the kids more stuff. Kids are smart enough to take advantage of this, as you well know. No kid is going to say, "Oh please, Daddy (or Mommy), don't buy me any more clothes or toys. Please let me help with the housework. Please, pretty please with sugar on top, let me pick up after myself!" If you do have such a child, light a candle in thanksgiving. Light two.

Taking away toys and other items that the other parent bought for the children is a surefire recipe for resentment. However, you could implement a rule that whenever a new toy or item comes home with your children, they have to pick one other item to give away or discard. I'm aware that not everyone reading this will be in the middle or upper-middle economic scale. Not every kid has too much stuff. Some children don't have enough stuff.

If you're so financially strapped that you can't buy many things for your children, don't penalize them just because the other parent can afford to buy them things. And don't feel down on yourself for the situation. (Easy words to write; tough advice to follow, I know.) Remember that one of the cardinal beliefs that clutterers need to change applies to everyone: Things do not equal love. You're doing the best you can with what you have. If you're giving them love, guidance, and understanding, that counts for a lot more than all the video games, movies, and toys in the world.

Now for some good news. If there are significant differences in attitudes about cluttering at the two homes, this can be turned into a positive advantage.

## If You're Not a Clutterer

If one parent is a clutterer and one isn't, this could be a great opportunity to drive home the fact that your rules about not-cluttering aren't just arbitrary. How better to explain to your children that cluttering is serious business? Have a frank discussion with them about the two lifestyles. Explain that living in a cluttered environment can cause stress and (if this is true) may have contributed to the divorce.

## If You Are a Clutterer

"I lived with Mom. It was more comfortable to be at her house. Being at Dad's is physically uncomfortable. When I am with my dad, I have problems being 100 percent relaxed. The space is new and doesn't feel like my own. It tends to be less comfortable."

—Tiffany,
from a divorced family

Have the same discussion, but, just as discussed earlier, tell your children that it's something you're working on. You could explain that people have different views on many things, including standards of neatness. Be honest. If you felt that your ex was way too neat, explain that that can be stressful too. Help them to choose a balance between your way of life and your ex's. There are pluses and minuses to every behavior. Even cluttering has a plus. A clutterer's house is usually more relaxed to be in. Sure, there are the extra stresses that cluttering causes, but the general atmosphere is more relaxed. Don't use that as an excuse for cluttering, but as an example of how different ways of living aren't all bad or all good. Balance is better.

## Your Children Can Be Your Allies

As a single parent, your parenting time is more limited and more valuable. Often your children will be quite aware of this and really be willing to help you out. They know you don't have time to pick up after them, and barely enough time to pick up after yourself. Sometimes, all they need is a little guidance on ways to keep clutter from coming into the house.

But please don't expect your children to be little adults. While it's normal and reasonable to expect your children to pitch in with the housework and taking care of their younger siblings, it's not fair to expect them to become housekeepers and nannies. I've heard from too many adults who attend Clutterless Recovery Groups that being expected to be the housekeeper may have resulted in a neater house when they were growing up, but ultimately was their justification for being cluttered adults when they grew up. Because cluttering in both adults and children is often an expression of rebellion, we want to turn not-cluttering into a way of life that we've chosen, not something imposed.

## Support Groups

Parents Without Partners (*www.parentswithoutpartners.org*) is open to all single parents. I can personally recommend them as a resource. Single parenting is a challenge, but you'll surely make it easier on yourself and your kids if you can discuss the challenges and solutions with others just like you. They provide international support meetings, discussions, professional speakers, study groups, publications, and social activities for families and adults.

# Okay, Let's Get Practical

So what can you do to keep your children sane and decluttered after visiting your cluttered ex? Let's assume the worst-case scenario. Your ex lets your children run free, like wild mustangs on the range. The positive side of this is that they learn that different people have different standards of living. No one likes living by the rules all the time.

With all the negative behaviors that divorced parents may exhibit, this may be one battle you shouldn't even try to fight. If parents are using their children as pawns in a chess game of getting even with each other, nobody wins. You may have to accept the occasional lapse in neat behavior as part of the deal. There will probably be bigger issues you won't be able to accept. Choose what is worth reacting to and what is not.

Karl Paul Reinhold Niebuhr, a 20th-century theologian and advocate of Christian Realism wrote a wonderful prayer on acceptance that most people have heard this part of: "God, give us grace to accept with serenity the things that cannot be changed, courage to change the things which should be changed and the wisdom to distinguish the one from the other." Your ex's cluttering behavior and the abandonment of your rules of behavior in regard to cluttering just aren't worth the fight.

You have very little control of what goes on at the other parent's house. As long as he or she is not mistreating your children or teaching them other values you don't approve of, such as drug use, promiscuity, or a lack of respect for authority, cluttering is a low priority. You already know that it might take from one to three days for children to adjust from one parenting style to the other.

Ease your children back into the routine around your house. While I don't advocate letting them clutter at will, you might overlook some minor cluttering the first day after they come home. They're still processing a lot from the visit. By the second day, you should be able to implement a normal way of life at home. It's important that kids, from preschoolers to teenagers, accept that their routine at home remains the same, even when they go away for awhile. They need the structure you provide. Despite what they may say, they want structure in their lives. Structure either gives them something to rebel against (for teens) or a sense of safety (all ages).

## Ease the Stress of Switching From One Household to Another

While there are going to be certain toys, games, videos, or CDs du jour that every kid feels he just has to cart from one house to the other, for the most part, try to have everything your children need at each house. This means two sets of clothes, shoes, toys, games, and so on, but it'll ease the stress on both the kids and the parents. Packing is stressful. I know few adults who have to travel for business who don't feel less stressed if they keep a packed bag of travel essentials and clothes. This was a major recommendation for road warriors in my book *Clutter-Proof Your Business*. It works for adults who travel for business. It works for me when I take my periodic cross-country seminar trips. It'll work for your kids.

## How Important Is It?

It's inevitable that your kids will forget something. Use this as an opportunity to teach one of the values essential to living an uncluttered life. Have them ask themselves, "How important is it?" Can they live without the item for a weekend? Can they find something else at the other house to amuse themselves with? Chances are, they can. In learning to be adaptable, they break the hold possessions have over them. In seeking alternatives, they learn to think creatively. And, most importantly, they learn that things are interchangeable. This will help later in life when it comes to discarding items that have outlived their usefulness.

You can't do this with schoolwork. Or can you? If they have to read three chapters in a certain science book, you just can't sidestep that. But if they have to do a report on something in that science book, this is a great opportunity to demonstrate that information is almost always available somewhere else or in a different form. The subject can be explored on the Internet or in other books, or they can find it at a trusty library. Even in this age of computers, real books at real libraries can open worlds to children. Remember your childhood joy wandering the stacks and finding books you'd never imagined? Here's your chance to pass that joy on to your children.

## What if They Don't Want to Follow the Rules When They Get Home?

This happens. Adults are the same way. After two weeks of unstructured vacation time in Hawaii, how much do you want to get back into your business clothing, fight rush-hour traffic, and return to a job where you're smarter than your boss? You do it because the reward of fitting back into the mold is worth it. So will your children, if they feel the rewards outweigh the drawbacks. Throughout this book, I've tried to make living a not-cluttering life seem like less of a chore and more of a way of life. Talk to your kids. Ask them if life isn't easier for them when they can find the clothes they want to wear, get their books ready for school, know where their toys are and concentrate on living life instead of looking for things. They may surprise you and accept these "adult" views.

Children are constantly making choices about how they want to live their lives. When they're very young, they generally choose to live a life that pleases their parents. As they grow older, they're more concerned about fitting in with their peers and finally about pleasing themselves. If you can teach them that living a life of not having to clutter will help them achieve those goals, you've done a good job. Now, if you could just do something about that boss...

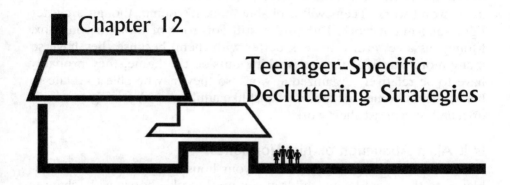

# Chapter 12

# Teenager-Specific Decluttering Strategies

*Don't lose your connection with your kids over messy rooms. Teach them as a consultant, or you could raise cluttered adults. It's a question of balance and playing for the long game.*

—Dr. Michael J. Bradley, Ed.D.,
psychologist specializing in the treatment of teens,
a parent, and author of *Yes, Your Teen Is Crazy!*
and *Yes, Your Parents Are Crazy*

Dr. Bradley hit the nail on the head during our interview with that statement. Although this book is ostensibly about teaching your children to declutter and not-clutter, the bigger picture is that it's about finding balance regarding cluttering—and life. The suggestions here will help to guide them onto the not-cluttering path, but if it comes down to a choice between having "neat" kids and having kids you can communicate with, choose the latter. Don't get too neurotic about having them live up to your standards of neatness.

## The Teenage Mind

Teens deserve their own chapter because they're different than younger kids in so many ways, even more so than the difference between preschool and middle-school children. Most of the preceding suggestions about rewarding your kids for decluttering or not-cluttering apply to teenagers: praise, poker chips, a reward system, and so on. The clutter dance most likely won't work. Teens will probably think it's dumb, though a clutter fight song might work. But you've still got a lot of tools in your box. Money, as a reward, will work better with them, because they have so many more wants. If they're working outside the home, they probably have to be relatively organized at work, so they may be able to relate to being neat at home—or they may, just like adults, use cluttering as a form of rebellion against their work.

## Is It Alien Abduction or Just Hormones?

While the 12- to 18-year-olds in your house may bear some resemblance to the sweet loving children you used to play horsie with, chances are that you are wondering if FBI agent Fox Mulder from *The X-Files* is right about alien abduction. Right off the bat, I want to acknowledge that most teens are good kids, who do well in school and in their social life and do not cause discord in their families (oh, a little stress now and then, but not major discord). Labeling all teens as disruptive is incorrect and counterproductive. People of all ages generally live up to, or down to, what's expected of them.

But it would be disingenuous not to recognize that, during their teen years, kids change. They're making the transition from children to young adults. Their brain chemistry and their entire bodily chemistry are changing. Their lives are seldom idyllic. They're under a lot of stress. More is expected of them, and they expect more from themselves. In learning to define themselves, they have to rebel. If they don't challenge their parents at this age, they'll carry this unresolved issue to their adult lives. You know all this. You were a teen once too (and you've probably learned that saying this to your own teens results in them rolling their eyes). But, of course, you weren't as much trouble as your teen. No, you were a model kid. Right? Yeah, so was I.

## Teens Have to Experiment

"Teens have to experiment with being neat to learn about it. Let them be disorganized and not be able to find something. Violating the rules is part of 'identity formation.'

When they violate what we want them to do, it's not a tragedy. It's part of the learning curve. If we stay calm, they can learn from it."

—Dr. Michael Bradley Ed.D, author of *Yes, Your Teen Is Crazy*! and *Yes, Your Parents Are Crazy*

If you insist that your teens keep neat, without their involvement, they'll see that as a point to rebel against later. If they understand that being neat can benefit them—being able to find things when they want them and being able to get off to school with all their books and papers with less hassle—they'll learn that being neat has intrinsic rewards.

When they can't find something, instead of finding it for them, let them do the searching. Enough aggravating times like that and it might dawn on them that, if they were a little more organized, they wouldn't have to go through the trouble of looking under piles of clutter every time they want something. We all learn more from our mistakes than from our easy successes.

"Paying the consequences for behavior is a sense of empowerment."

—Kim Arrington Cooper, M.Ed., marriage and family counselor

## Sublet Their Room

No, I don't mean that you should kick your teens out into the street and rent out their rooms. Dr. Michael J. Bradley had this idea to help teens to learn to not-clutter:

"Transfer ownership to the parent. The kid is subletting it. Take doors off closets. Kids don't understand closets. Put in shelves so they can put their TV, and so on, in it. It looks cool to them. Make their room like a studio apartment. Let the kids pick out their own carpet."

Sure, it might be something bizarre. So what? You're just the land-lord. You can rip it out when the current tenant moves out and put something sane in. Meanwhile, your teens are learning to "own" their rooms, and will be more likely to take care of it. When we "own" our living space, we also "own" our clutter.

While we're on the subject of rooms, let's talk about your being able to inspect them. It would be naive to ignore that there may be something more dangerous than smelly socks, such as drugs, hiding under those dirty clothes apparently tossed willy-nilly on the floor.

Dr. Bradley suggests handling it this way:

> "Conduct a negotiated inspection. There has to be a carrot for the kid. He gets XYZ. Kids may think their parents are neurotic about being neat. Say, 'I'm kind of neurotic about neatness. Can you help me?' Remember, you're playing for the long game. Keep the anger out of it."

## Yes, Their Brains Are Different

Just for the record, teens are different. Research in the 1990s has discovered that a teenager's brain is chemically different than a child's or an adult's brain. Traditional wisdom tells us that 95 percent of a person's brain has been developed when we are around 5 years old. That's true, but it's not the whole picture. While 95 percent of the brain's *mass* has developed by then, "the most advanced parts of the brain don't complete their development until adolescence is pretty much over," according to Dr. Michael J. Bradley, Ed.D.

This statement is based on research done by Dr. Jay Giedd, chief of brain imaging at the Child Psychiatry Branch of the National Institute of Mental Health, in conjunction with colleagues at UCLA and McGill University in Canada. These findings were confirmed by Dr. Deborah Yurgelun-Todd, a neuropsychologist at McLean Hospital in Belmont, Massachusetts. For details of these studies, and for some really excellent tools for understanding and dealing with difficult teenagers, read Dr. Bradley's book *Yes, Your Teen Is Crazy!*

The prefrontal cortex of the brain, which is the part that utilizes our most sophisticated human abilities such as decision-making, control of our emotions (no surprise for most parents there, that this area is under-developed in teens!), and control of impulses changes rapidly from about age 12 to about age 20. Thus, your teenagers' brains aren't completely developed until (with luck), they're out of the house. So, if you have trouble understanding your teens, it's not your fault. They are chemically unstable and changing daily. They don't know what's going on either.

## Every Parent's Nightmare

I was every parent's nightmare. I embraced rebellion with the ardor of an obsessed lover. Rules were anathema to me. Just say the word "rule," and I would find a way to break it. Even before I discovered drugs and alcohol as my preferred forms of rebellion, I found cluttering. The easiest sort of rebellion was to clutter. I could do it at home. I didn't have to do it so well that my peers were impressed with my bravado. It elicited a wonderful (from my standpoint) reaction from my parents and gave me the chance to define myself. *"All your silly rules about picking up my room are for conformists. I am an artist. I'm going to be a hippie when I grow up."* Then I'd storm out of the house, get on my motorcycle (later, after several near-fatal wrecks, this changed to my sports car) and go regale my peer group of other malcontents with my expression of independence. Cluttering was a great ally, sort of a silent partner in my rebellion conspiracy. It did its work of bugging my parents when I wasn't there to do it.

When I finally left the house and did become a hippie, there were no not-cluttering rules. I felt free. Only when I lived in a commune did I learn that every group needs some rules about making messes to ensure harmony. Communes failed as an experiment. There are lots of theories why, but mine is that no one would do the dishes or pick up their messes.

So when your teens are acting up and their clutter is driving you up the wall, you may be able to take some small comfort in the fact that you aren't raising me. Or yours may be worse. If so, God bless you. You'll both get through it. And even apparently troubled teens can turn into productive adults—if you call being a writer productive, or adult.

## How About a Little Good News?

"In order to get your teens to listen to you, treat them with respect. One simple technique is to make an appointment with them when you want to discuss something important.

Another simple thing you can do to aid communication is to talk to them at eye-level. If they're sitting, sit. A parent who's standing will come across as overbearing. Listen to them, and don't have your responses all figured out."

—Karen Griggs, M.F.T.

Despite appearances, teens really do value adult input and want to have structure in their lives. Outwardly, they may ignore everything you say, belittle your ideas, and break every rule in your household. But they're in flux—emotionally and chemically. They crave stability and need to challenge it. The best you can do is to learn to communicate, negotiate when appropriate, stand your ground when you need to, and get your point across without coming off as too much of an authoritarian figure. Gee, that all sounds easy, doesn't it?

Even the neatest children can change into the worst clutterers in their teenage years. If you've done your not-cluttering work well in the early years, this may not happen, but because it's early for this book to be a classic, there won't be any way to verify this. Perhaps the 20th edition will have some verifiable data on that.

Meanwhile, back on Earth, what are you going to do? Let's start with some good news! You've got more ways to motivate your teenagers than your younger children. With younger children, you might use their desire to please you (pretty much diluted by the teen years) and the concept that being neat is part of fitting into the family. Teens are more concerned with fitting in with their friends than being a part of the family.

You aren't going to change this, but you can turn it to your advantage. You're still the adult. You're smarter than your teens. It's a simple fact that experience and age always outweigh inexperience and youth.

## Help Your Teens Want to Organize Their Schoolwork

Teacher after teacher told me that cluttered kids turn their schoolwork in late or incomplete. While your kids may not make the connection between being disorganized or cluttered and the D they got in English, you can help them understand the correlation. But do it gently. Yelling or belittling them for being cluttered has a snowball's chance in Hades of succeeding. You're the adult. Use some adult psychology to outwit, I mean to guide, them.

Whether your teenagers love school or hate it, you can motivate them to be more organized. There are two paths to the same destination of getting them to be more organized. Following are two examples you can use to get them to listen to you. You'll probably think of others. The whole point is to communicate with them and try to understand where they're coming from. They just might listen to you. Sit down with them and start a dialogue.

## Try a Conversation Instead of Telling Them What to Do

Try saying, "School sucks, doesn't it? How'd you like to fix it so you spend less time on it?"

Or you can say, "You seem to like school. How'd you like to make it easier on yourself?"

Either of these will get their attention. You aren't telling them to do something, you're offering to show them some great adult secret. You can embellish either statement with a story about how you hated/loved school and found out the secret of productivity. It may help to put it into the anecdotal realm, rather than having it come from you. Maybe you could say you learned it from someone else your teen might respect—a brother, sister, or other relative. Or you can tell them about a secret that your parent or some other adult shared with you. For some teens, that will work better, because it has nothing to do with you (after all, your IQ dropped 40 points when they turned 12). And, although no adult is as smart as a teen, ones other than their parents seem to have held onto a few more brain cells. It'd be really great if some sports figure, rock star, or actor ever confessed to being cluttered and that this secret helped them get through school. I haven't read one who has, but who knows? Maybe you will.

"Yeah?" they might grunt.

"Yeah. The deal is, when a person spends less time looking for stuff, he has more time to do what's important to them." (By putting things into the third person, and calling them a person instead of a kid, you're more likely to get their attention. *You* aren't telling *them* what to do.)

"Most people waste a lot of time because they can't find the information they need. They may be adept at researching at the library or on the Internet, but when they need to incorporate that information into a report or project, they can't find it. This happens at work all the time." By telling them that it happens to adults, it takes it out of the teen realm into the world they're trying to get into.

"Here's the secret. Successful people do all their work in one place. They have a desk or table that's theirs just for work or study. People who try to study in front of the TV and then take their books and papers back to their desk invariably lose or misplace something." (This might get them out of the living room.)

"If they have to go to the library to do research, they keep the research separate, in a binder all by itself. That way, they don't waste a lot of time looking for it when they're ready to use it. If they're doing Internet research, they don't print everything." (You sneaky devil, you. You've planted a seed that will keep paper clutter from growing. Aw heck, you're saving a tree or two too.) "They save the information they're going to use so they can cut and paste it into their documents. Saving Web pages is a waste of time. They do save the link at the top of the text document, so they can reference it if they have to."

This should make sense to the teen. Teens like to think they are efficient.

## AD/HD Techniques

The chapter devoted to AD/HD has a lot of specific suggestions. For your teen with AD/HD, this conversation will help specifically with schoolwork to help him enhance his learning:

"You know, one of the brightest guys at the office seems to wander around the halls a lot. He says that movement helps him think. He doesn't file things the same way as everyone else, but he's developed a system of making things visible, yet neat, that works for him. He uses clear plastic crates to keep items he's working on at the moment together. He says that if he files things in a filing cabinet, he forgets where they are. It's like they cease to exist. He found that trying to keep everything on his desktop was inefficient. He spent too much time shuffling papers. He keeps a radio going in his office at a low volume so as not to disturb others." (You can try this subterfuge, but volume means something different to all teens than it does to adults.) He says the background noise filters out the noise in his head."

You'll probably come up with even more applicable scenarios as time goes on. Fit them into your own teen's world.

## Turn Those Hormones Into an Asset

Whether you've decided to allow your teens to date, or are considering sending them to a cloister or monastery until they're 18, dating will be on their minds. This is a good thing for you. It's a most valuable tool in your not-cluttering collection. This whole book is about the "why" of cluttering, so use the "why" to effect the "how-to."

The following suggestions are boy-girl specific. I don't think they are sexist. Boys and girls have different ways of relating to the opposite sex. Whether your family approves of boy-girl visits to their rooms is up to you, but for many (often with the door welded open) families this is common. Sharing a kitchen or dining-room table for studying probably doesn't threaten any parents, and can lead to having a neater house. If your rules are that it's okay to invite boys/girls over as long as they stay in the common family rooms, you can modify this strategy by skipping the first paragraph and saying instead:

> "It's good that your boyfriend can come over and study with you. Of course, he could be reading more information about you than you intended when he sees the messy living room."
>
> "Huh?"
>
> "Yeah. I'll let you in on a little secret..."

Then follow the example below.

## For Girls

> "Janie, I know that your room is your sanctuary, and you can keep it as neat or as messy as you want within reason." (Approaching the subject like that gives her a sense of control—"sanctuary," without abnegating your parental overrides—"within reason.") "The habits you develop now are going to carry through into your adult life. Do you buy that?" (It's always a good idea to ask them questions, just to make sure they're listening. And asking questions that can easily be answered with a yes sets the stage for agreement.)
>
> "Yeah, I guess so."
>
> "Good. Then I'll let you in on a little secret." ('Oh, boy,' she might think, 'some adult secret.') "Most guys get turned off by sloppy

girls. They see a messy room and think less of you. If a guy is serious about a relationship, he's not going to want to get into one with someone who's going to trash the house."

"I don't care. If a guy doesn't like me for who I am, then I'm not interested. I'm not going to change for anyone." (This is a highly illogical response, but a likely one. Teenagers think they're individuals, but are really more concerned with fitting in than being themselves. They don't even know who they are yet.)

"Sure, I understand that. Think about it this way. If you go out with a boy whose car is full of junk, doesn't that make you think that he doesn't respect you enough to even clean out his car for a date? Don't you get the impression he's a self-centered chauvinist and not someone you want to get to know better? It's the same with your room, and later, your apartment. How you live makes a statement. A guy would think the same way. Would you want to marry a guy who's sloppy and expects you to pick up after him all the time?"

"Well, no, I don't want to spend my life picking up after some guy, that's for sure." (It's highly unlikely that you'll get any other response to this.)

The following scenario can be modified for your daughters as well, however the focus should probably be the same as the example above. The first paragraph is boy-specific, although not always. Today's world is different than the one we grew up in.

## For Boys

Do you remember those optical illusion cartoons titled something such as, "What's on every man's mind?" On one level, they showed a bald-headed, bearded guy looking thoughtful. The more you looked at it, you began to see that it was really a picture of a curvy fantasy woman. It should be no secret that behind your boy's forehead, images of girls are clogging his brain cells and interfering with the synapses between cells, impairing efficient functioning. Some boys even grow to be men and overcome this obsession. Most of us don't.

Use this fact of life to your advantage. But also be aware that what's gone on in your house up to now may make your words sound hollow. If you have a two-parent home and the wife does all the housework, you're going to have a hard time convincing Junior that picking up and housework aren't "women's work." If they've grown up in that sort of environment, they're likely to view their sloppiness as a normal male attribute. The best way to change this is to have Dad start doing some housework and picking up. Sorry guys. You could weasel your way out of this by pointing out that you keep your tools and the garage neat and tidy, but that's only a half-measure.

The easiest way to convince teenage boys that cleanliness is important is to start with their car (or the family car, if they don't have their own). Fortunately, guys already know that their wheels are an important part of their identity and are likely to wash, wax, and clean them anyway. This gives you a leg up on teaching them why they shouldn't clutter. If, with a vehicle, being neat will impress the girls, then you can use this as a segue into keeping their rooms neat for the same reason.

"Got a date this Saturday?"

"Yeah."

(If the answer is no, there's still hope. "Going cruising?" applies equally.)

"Have fun." (Say this even if you mean to have good clean fun and are fearful that his idea of fun is vastly different from yours. As long as the evening doesn't end with flashing lights from a police car, you both win.) "I guess one thing that hasn't changed about girls is that they're more attracted to a guy with a clean car than to a guy who doesn't seem to care."

"I guess."

"Why do you think that is?"

"I dunno. Girls are weird."

"Yep. I agree with that. But you know what? Girls are more complicated than us guys." (Okay, you're sneaking in a little male bonding. Do it when you can.) "To them, being neat means that you respect them. And, as far as I can figure out," (a bemused grin at this point wouldn't hurt) "that's the first step to their heart."

"I guess."

"So, you've got the car all cleaned out? Vacuumed? Washed? Waxed?"

"Yeah."

"That'll do the trick. You know, if you want to invite a girl over to study sometime that would be okay."

"Yeah, that'd be okay, I guess."

"Of course, the same principle applies to the house (or your room) as to the car. If it's messy, she won't like it. Like you said, girls are weird."

"Yeah, I guess so."

"Well, I'll leave it up to you. You might want to straighten up a little bit if you want to impress her."

Leave it there. You've planted a seed. Let it sprout.

## Teens Test Limits

You already know that a big part of being a teenager is defining themselves. To do that, they need to question the boundaries they've grown up with. Sometimes, if you say something's black, they'll have to say it's white just because they need to show that they're independent. A kid who's grown up being relatively neat may start cluttering. We're back to the control issue. They want to be in control of what they do, what they own, and where they put it. Picking up seems dumb. Why make the bed if you're going to sleep in it in a few hours and mess it up again?

Tammy, a teenager, told me this:

> "I didn't place any value on being neat until my friends started saying things like, 'Look at all the cool stuff,' in my room. I could tell by their tone of voice and body language that what they really meant was, 'What a mess.' When I went to visit them, their houses were a lot neater and their rooms were much different than mine. It made me think. It convinced me to stop being so messy."

The best tool you have to convince your teens that keeping uncluttered has value is peer pressure. Encourage them to invite their friends over. I can't guarantee that this will make them keep their rooms up to military standards, but it certainly won't hurt and will, more often than not, help.

If your teenagers have decided that the family room is the place for their discarded jerseys, tossed books, and dirty dishes, they're testing the family limits. Yelling at them only causes stress for both of you—more stress than the mess. Could you turn this into a tool to help you?

## Stress Mess

If you're not a clutterer, become one for awhile. Fortunately, for most of you, it'll be easier for you to mess a little bit than it will be for a clutterer to not mess. If doing a little bit of controlled cluttering causes you a lot of stress, you may be a little obsessive about neatness. This could be a good thing to learn, as you probably never thought of yourself that way. It could be a chance to learn balance. Start strewing your clothes, books, and magazines around the family room. Leave some dishes on the coffee table. It won't take long for your teen to notice that something's different.

"Mom, this room is a mess."

"Really? I hadn't noticed."

"Yeah, what's gotten into you?"

"I dunno (a little teen-speak comes in handy), I just don't feel like picking things up."

"Well, it's gross. I wanted to invite some friends over to watch a video tonight, but I'd be embarrassed."

"I guess so. What do you think we should do about it?"

"Why don't you clean up your mess?"

(Avoid shouting, 'Why don't you clean up yours?') "I guess I could. But it's hard to clean up part of a mess. Why don't we each pick up our own stuff?"

If your teen balks at this, saying she has something more important to do, then just say, "Okay, we'll just leave it. When did you say your friends are coming over?"

If you've enlisted your teen's cooperation, you might throw in some wisdom about how much easier it would have been to not have made the mess in the first place, or how easy it is to be messy once the room is messy. Without hitting your kid over the head, you can make a big point on the value of not-cluttering.

Do this a few times, and, if your teens are social, they'll probably start picking up after themselves.

## If They Have a Job Outside the Home

If this were the last century, they'd be expected to have a job. Today it's more of a choice, depending on your family's financial situation. Working, in my opinion, is good for kids, as long as it's not so much that it takes away from their schoolwork. It can help them learn to not-clutter, as few workplaces where they're likely to end up are going to allow a lot of the creative cluttering that adults get away with.

If they're still cluttering up the family area, or not putting their laundry out, it's perfectly fair to warn them that if they don't improve these habits, you'll give them a bill for housekeeping services. Then do it. No kid wants to waste his money on something like that when there are more important things to waste his money on.

Working could give them one of two reactions towards their cluttering at home. They could wish to emulate a boss or coworker who's neat or see that neatness really makes work (and schoolwork) flow more easily. The other reaction is that they could clutter more, because they "just don't have time to declutter" or because they think their job is lame and, just like adults, may use cluttering as an expression of their independence from their job.

If the first scenario is operative in your house, count yourself among the chosen. If the second is going on, you'll have to work at stemming this behavior now so they won't carry it forward into their adult life. If their cluttering just started when they got the job, you've got a pretty good idea of what's going on. If they've always been clutterers, you can use the work-clutter technique to help with other areas of their life.

"You like your job okay?"

"I guess."

"Like your boss?"

"She's okay." (If you're really lucky, you'll get, 'She's, like, a total jerk.' That could open more doors of communication.)

"Yeah, most bosses are sorta okay, but they can all be jerks at times."

Your teen may or may not respond to this little bit of communication opening. If he does, go with the flow, but remember to work cluttering into the conversation somehow. Otherwise this will end up in some unrelated pool of parent-child discussion.

"I suppose you have to keep your workplace area all picked up, don't you?"

"Yeah."

"Why do you think that is?"

"Cuz they have stupid rules."

"Yeah. I have to put up with a lot of stupid rules at work, too. But, stupid or not, every workplace has rules. I don't think that's going to change as long as we work for other people. I hate to admit it, but those rules do make things go more smoothly. Wouldn't you agree?"

"I guess."

"Sure. At least you don't have to pick up the clutter from the other kids who work there. That's a good thing, isn't it?"

"Yeah, it is. Some of those kids are real slobs. I hate coming into a dirty workplace. Work's lame enough as it is."

"Most of us feel the same way. You know what? Don't you think your mom and I feel the same way when you don't pick up?" (Okay, you trapped him using some logical progression. Don't gloat.)

"Well, I guess it's kind of similar."

"Hey, I know how it is. You work, go to school, try to have a social life. It's hard to find the time to pick up stuff, isn't it?"

"It sure is. There's never enough time."

"I agree with that. But, you know, I've been thinking. I waste a lot of time when I can't find something because I didn't put it back where it belonged. That ever happen to you?"

"I guess you're right. I do spend a lot of time rummaging through my stuff."

"We both do. What worked for me was to force myself to put stuff away. It seemed like a big hassle, but it took less time than trying to find it later. Why don't you try that?"

I wish I could follow this with a statement like, "Oh gee, Dad! You're a genius. I'll start doing that right away." If I did, you'd know I'd flipped out. But you might get something like, "Could be. I might try that." If you get a response at least *that* positive, you've won. Actually, both of you have won.

But don't stop there. The next time your kid drops something where it doesn't belong, say something like, "Reckon (if you're not from the South, try "Suppose") you'll be able to find that again when you want it?"

Don't nag or go on forever about the conversation you had about dropping stuff where it doesn't belong. Your kid remembers it. Short sentences communicate. Long sentences preach. Preaching is a profession; it's not parenting.

# In Conclusion

Teen clutter is a bigger challenge than little kid clutter. Teens have more stuff. They have more on their minds and don't think things through. Most of the decluttering and not-cluttering information in this book will help you deal with their general cluttering.

They may have been neat as little kids and turned into clutterers when they crossed the threshold into being teens. Ideally, you'll be able to apply the lessons in this chapter to help get them back on track. But, if nothing seems to work and your attempts cause more stress than ease, you'll either have to rethink your methods of communicating or reevaluate what's really important. If your biggest teen-raising challenge is cluttering, then count your lucky stars and let it go. It's not worth inserting a wedge in your relationship. *People* win out over *things* any day. Ask yourself, what's really important?

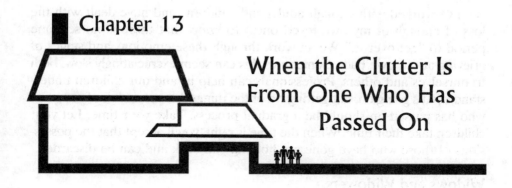

# Chapter 13

# When the Clutter Is From One Who Has Passed On

*My cluttering has escalated since my husband's death. I was sleeping 14–18 hours a day after that. It's really hard to make much of a mess when you aren't fully functional and are either sleeping or sleepwalking. I probably wasn't a model homemaker before that, but it was nothing like what it is now. Part of the clutter is my late husband's belongings that I couldn't sell or throw away then. I wasn't functional enough to make the necessary effort to even give anything away. Now, 7 years later, I've just gotten to the point where I can give stuff away and have also started going through his extensive files, which were useless, because they were so old and never necessary to keep in the first place. The problem is that I can only do it in small time increments, and I have to be really psyched up to start.*

—B.A., from an e-mail

## Death and Clutter

If you're a widow or widower or have suffered the loss of a child, you and your children will have some special cluttering challenges. Your children may react to the loss of a loved one in different ways as far as cluttering is concerned. They may become more acquisitive and fearful of letting things go, or they may become ruthless about getting rid of things. The former is more likely, just as it is with an adult.

I've worked with enough adults and children (and have dealt with the loss of enough of my own loved ones) to know that there is no set time period to "get over it." We all work through these emotions and stages of grieving at our own pace. Sometimes this can seem excruciatingly slow, both to ourselves and others. Professionals can help us and our children understand what's going on, but getting rid of the things that remind us of someone who has passed on should be a gradual process. Take your time. Let your children take their time. When the time is right, you'll accept that the possessions of those who have gone are holding you back and can be discarded.

## Widows and Widowers

People don't leave us when they pass on. Their memories are always with us. Coping with grief is an individual thing. Some people seem to do it better than others, at least on the outside. Sometimes parents feel like they have to put up a strong front for their children when they feel anything *but* strong. Sometimes well-meaning friends and relatives push survivors to move on with their lives. They say that you should get rid of the clothing and possessions of your partner, often before you're ready. I've worked with many adults who felt angry with those who hurried them, angry with their partner for dying on them, and angry with themselves for not "getting over it" as everyone else seemed to think they should.

Do what you can, when you can. One thing that worked for me and has been used by other clutterers is something such as this: After I'd dealt with my own clutter to a large extent, I learned how to let go of my attachments to my own stuff. I also learned to appreciate how good it felt to let go, versus how bad I had told myself it would feel. We hold onto things because we fear that the letting go will be more painful than the holding on. This is false, but that doesn't make it any less real to us.

## If Your Child Has Passed On

Probably nothing you do in your life will be harder than decluttering the room of a child who has gone. The little keepsakes you treasure such as drawings and cards that you already have stored away should probably be left alone. You need them. A whole room devoted to the memory of your child may be too much, but if you don't need the room and the trauma of clearing it out is too much for you, let it be.

More important than having a decluttered house is having peace. If knowing that things are just as your child left it comforts you, be glad for that comfort. If it is bothering you or your other children, then you can choose to do something about it. Don't do this alone, and don't do it until you're ready. As Hippocrates said, *"First, do no harm."* If your other children could use the space for themselves, then consider making the room a gift from the child who is gone to those who are here. She would want you to.

If you're ready, read the following story. The principles are the same. You cannot and should not do this alone. Once you've gotten permission from your child to let her things go, imagine the smiles of happiness that those same possessions will bring to other children. Those smiles will help you keep going.

# How I Did It

I'd carted an entire roomful of my father's and mother's possessions across the country, to my home. After I'd been practicing the Clutterless way of life for many months, I was ready to reclaim that space. First, I prayed for guidance and strength. Prayer helps us feel less alone and isolated. Then I called my clutter buddy and told her what I was about to do. That way I had two clutter buddies—God and another clutterer. If you don't have a clutter buddy, call any understanding, nonjudgmental friend. If you don't have a friend, you can call me. Doing any decluttering alone is tough. Doing this kind of decluttering alone is next to impossible.

When I went into my parents' clutter room, I mentally envisioned them. I said, "Mother and Father, you know I love you, and I know you love me. I've kept these things to remind me of you. Now I'm strong enough to keep your memory without needing all these possessions. With your permission, I'd like to lovingly release them." I waited, and, while I didn't hear a voice from beyond say, "Sure, Sonny, toss away," I didn't hear them say no, either.

As I went through the boxes, it was easy to see what was junk. The exuberant entireties from Ed McMahon to reenter the Publisher's Clearing House Sweepstakes from 1975 didn't even merit consideration. So it was with most of the clutter they (mostly my mother) had accumulated.

There were some powerful memories mixed in with the junk. As I worked, ghosts swirled out of the boxes, like an image from *Raiders of the Lost Ark* when the Ark of the Covenant was opened. Some were pleasant and some were frightening. I cried, felt emotions I thought I'd forgotten about, and went on. You can too—if you're ready. If it's too daunting, stop immediately. Call your buddy and talk about it. This may be too painful to do in one try, but if you can, the rewards will be tremendous. They were for me. You've been holding on to those things for years. If you have to walk away and come back another day, they'll still be there. It may take you several tries, but you can do it, when you're ready to do it.

I kept important things in three new boxes labeled "memories." I came across pictures of me as a child. Naturally I kept those! I was a cute kid, if I do say so myself—and so innocent looking! I read letters from my father that made him more human, and, I hate to admit it, more like me than I had perceived him in real life. Mother had kept letters I'd written her from my Amazon jungle-exploring days. She even kept some adolescent short stories and poems I'd written. With my newly critical eye, I was able to discern that a poet I wasn't and did know it. They got tossed.

There were hundreds of photos, mostly of my parents with people I didn't know. Those I discarded. I did save a few photos of them alone, or of them and my sister or me. I'd learned from my own decluttering to discern what has value and what doesn't and to trust my instincts. When I moved from Los Angeles back to Texas, I carried those three boxes instead of the 600 pounds of junk. I felt lighter—physically and spiritually. I seldom go back to those boxes. But I know where they are. That gives me comfort. That, my friends, is what memory possessions are supposed to do—comfort us, not weigh us down.

## The Difference Between Memory Possessions and Clutter

A woman came to one of my workshops, brought by her adult daughter. I told this story on Dr. Laura Schlessinger's show, and Dr. Laura agreed with what I told the lady. The mother approached me at the break. Her cluttering issue wasn't her whole house, like most of the attendees.

"I live in a 4,000-square-foot house. I have kept a lot of my deceased husband's things. My daughter is after me to get rid of them. But I just can't."

Mr. Clutter Expert, here, envisioned at least 2,800 of those square feet to be filled with boxes and boxes of her husband's possessions. But instead of assuming I knew everything (always a good idea), I asked her how much stuff there was.

"It's awful. Almost half of the walk-in closet is full of boxes of his stuff."

Most clutterers would thank their lucky stars if their only clutter problem was half of a walk-in closet.

"Well, it doesn't take a psychiatrist to understand that you're holding onto these things of his as a reminder of him. Have you been able to get rid of anything that belonged to him?" I asked.

"Oh yes, I got rid of most of his clothes and all of his tools within the first year of his passing. I donated his furniture to Goodwill. All that's left are a dozen boxes of personal items and the suit he wore when we got married."

"Ma'am (I can't help it, I'm a Southern boy), it's normal to want to keep some things that belonged to someone we love. Your daughter loves you and thinks she's doing the right thing. But it sounds to me like you've done a good job. You've decided what you could let go of and what you cannot. The only question I have for you is, does it make you sad when you see those boxes and suit in the closet?"

"Oh no! I get a warm feeling and remember the wonderful times we had."

"Then, if you want my opinion, those items are not clutter. They are memory possessions. If the time comes that you want to get rid of them, do it. But until then, keep them."

This insight from a third party brought peace to both the mother and the daughter. It gave me a sense of the value of what I do. We all won big that day. The daughter realized that she was, out of love, trying to control her mother's life, and the mother realized that she had a right to feel the way she felt. If only all mother-daughter issues were that easy to solve.

Keeping everything just as our loved ones left it is not healthy. Keeping a reasonable amount of keepsakes is human.

## Traumatic Events Can Precipitate Cluttering Behavior

Often, people will turn into full-fledged clutterers after a traumatic life event. The loss of a child, spouse, or parent could trigger cluttering behavior in adults and children. It doesn't have to be the death of a loved one. Sometimes the loss of a job can be traumatic for the adult, and the children will pick up on it. These life losses paralyze us, and paralysis can result in cluttering.

We can't implement organizing rules when our hearts are breaking and our brains are numb. The clutter becomes our defense against the loss.

We use the clutter, in this case, not to keep people out of our lives, as is so common, but to prevent any more sense of loss. If we don't discard anything, we don't lose it. We don't want to lose any more.

Coping mechanisms are like people—none are perfect. But they'll do for the time being. Both you and your children can learn to discard an occasional item together. You'll probably feel sadness when you get rid of something, no matter how insignificant it might seem to an outsider. But with every item you discard, with every clear space you create, you get stronger. Cry together if you need to. Have a ceremony for each item tossed or given away. In fact, give things away whenever possible. That way you are passing the memories of it on to someone new. That feels better, emotionally, than throwing something in the trash.

## Hope Springs From Despair

The following story came to me via e-mail from a clutterer who wishes to remain anonymous. While it is heartrending, it is typical. And it offers hope. The real reason I write these books is to help people find hope that they can change. I don't do it alone. Sometimes my spirituality speaks through me, and sometimes others allow me to voice their experiences. Clutterers are my family. We can overcome our cluttering (and help our children overcome it) when we realize what's behind it. Here's what the e-mail said:

> "My husband died 8 years ago, and, for the first 3–4 years, I was numb and didn't notice the chaos and clutter that was engulfing me. It also hadn't built up to the intense levels that screamed 'get the health department—quick!' that it eventually got to before I was motivated to do something about it.
>
> "What I think is happening for me now is that I'm relearning to be less clutter-oriented than I had been. (If the truth be told, I've never been a neatness freak.) It's as if I had learned the habit of being slovenly and now I have to learn to be more in tune with my surroundings. I don't want be the one that makes the efforts to keep my home more well kept, but there's no one except me to do it. (Well, there is my son, but he's not going to be a resource in this!)
>
> "So I'm forcing myself to go through a drawer and really clean it out, or a file folder or whatever, and purge, purge,

purge! I'm trying to be more consistent in my efforts but I'm not taking on projects one right after another. I guess that I have to rest up between them! What I had been doing was, when I came across something, no matter what, I couldn't make the decision to toss it, so it would be put back in some pile on some horizontal surface with the myriad other stuff. I've now started to be good about applying the rule that whatever I bring in, there has to be something that goes out, unless it's going to be consumed (such as food). What I'm in the process of clearing out is the accumulation from when I was in the throes of being grief-struck brain-dead."

If this story struck a cord in you, God bless you. I wish I could come to your house, hug you, and help you start your healing journey. I can't. All I can do is help you make yourself aware of what's really going on. You'll deal with this as you know is best for you. If clutter is your or your children's only defense against feeling loss, then give yourselves a break. Proceed slowly. Don't toss your possessions willy-nilly just because they are clutter. If your child is using this as a coping mechanism, help her learn new and better ones.

When you're ready, start going through your loved one's things. You may want to enlist the aid of your children. But only do this if they have apparently adapted to the loss. Doing this type of decluttering will bring you and your children closer together than you can imagine. Having another person there will ease the burden of decision-making. Your children will have their own ideas of what memory possessions they want to keep. Let them decide and don't second-guess them, unless they want to keep everything. This is all about letting go.

Set aside a whole day for this project. Take breaks. Go out for ice cream. It's not going to be easy, so pick a time when there aren't other conflicts going on. Be ready for some tears. Mainly, don't lose sight of the joy of letting go. Remember that you aren't discarding a person. You are discarding things.

Often, we tend to idealize those who are gone. My mother turned my father into the nicest man who ever walked the earth. My recollections were somewhat different. If your deceased hasn't attained sainthood yet, try to start with those items that were important to him, but that you didn't particularly care for. His mechanic's or shop tools? Her cookbooks and recipes? Once you start the flow of discarding, it turns from a trickle into a stream and, finally, into a river. It'll be easier to flow with the current if you start with the little things. If you build up the momentum slowly, when you get into the tougher items, they won't seem so daunting.

When you get to the things that have monetary value, keep the vision of how they can help others at the forefront. Whether you elect to give them away or sell them doesn't matter. What matters is that you are passing them on to where they will continue the memory of the one who used them.

## Unexpected Memories

One of the nicest things that happened to me was getting an e-mail from an old girlfriend's lover when she died. Though it may have been painful for him, he stood outside of himself and went through Toby's address book and let everyone know she was gone and when the service would be. Had it not been for his kindness, I would never have known. This notice enabled me to grieve and, curiously, to reestablish my memories of Toby. It enabled me to delete her from my own mailing list instead of one day getting a returned e-mail, never knowing what had happened.

As life would have it, I got three e-mails about friends who died last year. I guess it's a sign of the times.

## What if You Discover Secrets?

Whether in computer files or piles of papers, you may run across something that you didn't know about. Some of these things will be good news, such as a secret stash of money, stocks, or property, in which case, consider it a belated gift. Some of it may be of the nature you didn't want to know about. Immediately shred, delete, or otherwise purge these items. They serve no purpose but to cause hurt if you hold onto them. If a file even starts to look like something you don't want to know about, get rid of it. Let the dead rest in peace and let yourself go on in peace.

# In Conclusion

Letting go is hard. Your memories will not disappear when the things a person accumulated in his life go out the door. Hard as it is, when you do get rid of those things, you will open your life up for new experiences and people to come in. Cluttering is holding on to the past. Decluttering is opening the door to the future. May your life be filled with open doors.

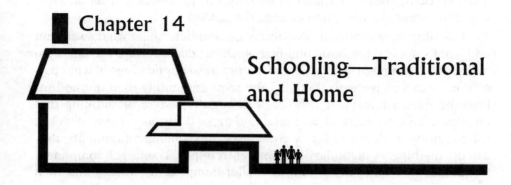

# Chapter 14

# Schooling—Traditional and Home

*We teachers, especially of young children, have to spend a lot of time teaching them organizational skills. If the parents could do that at home, they'd give their kids a head start in their schooling.*

—Karen Wiggins, Ph.D.,
school counselor

## More Than Being Neat and Tidy

"My kids' attitudes towards organization changed when they got into school. They took better directions. I think this is because they saw everybody else cleaning and being as organized as little kids can be."

—Trudy,
mother of six

Shhh! Don't tell your kids, but when you teach them how to stay uncluttered, you're really helping them to do better in school and life.

Until we achieve the genius level (about the teenage years) and can make independent breakthroughs, everything we learn builds on the habits we've learned. Being messy is a habit. Learning not to clutter is a habit. Help your kids break the first and embrace the second.

Learning to prioritize, make decisions, and determine what's relevant and what's not are the basic building blocks of decluttering, staying organized, and learning in school. These are practical applications of what psychologists call convergent thinking, the most commonly used method for learning most subjects. It's the logical, cognitive style of thinking that enables us to learn to read, do math, and make decisions. If your children (or an adult) can learn to break large tasks into smaller components, they can do anything. A dictionary is a perfect example. The larger component (language) is broken down into a smaller component (words) and then into even smaller parts (syllables), followed by putting them all back together again (the Humpty Dumpty approach to learning), using whole words as definitions.

Frederika Kotin, Ph.D., who has been a teacher for years and now works with troubled kids, had this to say about being disorganized and learning:

> "Cluttered kids turn in school work late. If a child is disorganized and has to dig through lots of papers to find things, it disrupts the way they relate to others and their subjects. It creates a state of anxiety.
>
> "Children need rules, but ignore the small stuff, it's not worth your time."

## Key Points

- Make a space to study.

- Declare that space sacred and it will keep itself neat (almost).

- Prioritizing and making decisions are part of the learning and the not-cluttering process.

- Breaking things into manageable components makes them easier.

- Keeping notes together makes it easier to stay organized.

## Make a Space to Study
### *A Brief Note to Disadvantaged Families*

Where your children study depends a lot on your family's economic level. People in the middle economic class assume that those from disadvantaged homes have the same things they consider essential. Not so. If you're a concerned parent and not from the middle and upper income levels, I congratulate you for having invested your money in buying this book or having checked it out of the library. Disorganization is even more of a challenge for you, simply because you don't have a lot of space to work with and may actually have to make do, make it last, or do without. For some of us clutterers, that's a trait we carry over from our upbringing, even when it's no longer true for us.

> "I used to tell kids in my class to study at the dining-room table if they didn't have a desk in their room. One day, a girl came up to me and said she didn't have a dining room or a dining-room table. She and her two sisters shared a bedroom in a four-room house. I did a little research and found that many disadvantaged families don't eat at tables. They eat on TV trays in front of the television. My middle-class upbringing had nothing to do with the realities in these families. What I tell them now is to take their TV trays into their bedroom so they can have a place to study. It doesn't matter where you study, what matters is that you have a specific place to study."
>
> —Linnelle,
> a public school teacher

An NPR radio show reported that, in lower-income families, the kitchen table is last on the list of acquisitions, after a TV, VCR, stereo, sofa. Many families in America live in two- or three-room houses, regardless of how many people are in the family. Thus, the likelihood of children from these families having their own room in which to study is about as likely as a clutterer passing up a bargain.

Children take pride in having their own area. If the best you can do is to get them their own TV tray or plastic table, then you've done the best you can do. To them, that's just as valuable as a "student" desk that richer families can provide. The important thing is that their study area be one they can call their own. If they have to take their work off it and put it away every night, it's even more valuable, in one sense. Economy has forced them to take care of their things. If you can give your child a crate or a sturdy box for their books and a shelf for supplies, you've given them all they need to apply the techniques in the rest of this chapter.

### Now for the Middle Class and Families With Greater Advantages

One reason children clutter is because they haven't learned to differentiate between space and place. If they have their own room to study in, it can only be their space if they make it so. But within that space, there is a place that's meant solely for studying. That means it's normal to have stuff, posters, and various things in it that make it theirs. What they need to absorb is that the study area is different than the rest of the room. If they have a desk, that desk is *only* for study materials and, probably, a computer.

If your children like to study in the family room or at the kitchen table, that's just fine. The important thing is to declare one area as a study area and then stick with it.

> "We stress to parents to have a place in the house where they can do their homework. Have kids do homework where parents can make eye contact. Set a specific time for homework. For instance, you could cook dinner, even if the whole family doesn't eat all at the same time. That would be a good time to study. Set a routine—every day at 5 or 6 will do fine."
>
> —Karen Wiggins, Ph.D.,
> school counselor

Learning this habit of making a place sacred is the biggest not-cluttering lesson there is. A sacred space is used only for the designated purpose, and only items related to that purpose go on it. Without sacred spaces, what happens with adults happens with kids. Unless an area is designated *sacred*, it becomes *miscellaneous*. And we all know how well "miscellaneous" files work in our offices. They rank in relevancy right behind the "to do TODAY!!!" (with a lot of smiley faces) folder.

## Declare That Space Sacred

Keep your children's learning modalities (visual, kinesthetic, verbal, or logical) in mind. Ask each one how they want to arrange their study area. Make it easy for them to get to the materials they need: books, supplies, research material, computer programs, and so on. If they feel like they're creating their own space, the way they want it, they're more likely to use it and keep it neat. If you design the space without their input, they're less likely to take pride in it. This is an important point, so don't gloss it over. Sure, it would be much easier and faster if you just went in and put up shelves, bought desks and tables, and declared everything sacred from on high. It will have about as much chance of succeeding as decluttering for them and then nagging them to keep it neat.

You have to keep your real goal in mind here. It's to make your children feel like they're part of the process, so that they'll want to keep the process going. If they understand that the "system" of organizing is of their own devising, they'll be more likely to follow it.

A bookshelf is pretty standard, regardless of the way a child learns. Books belong on shelves. So does clear space. There needs to be enough clear space on the bookshelf to make it obvious when books are out of place. Instead of cramming books on one shelf, make a space in the middle for clear space. It's unlikely that one child will have so many books that she'll use the complete unit. If two kids have to share a bookshelf, it could be a good opportunity for the cluttering child to see the difference of how a neater sibling makes use of space.

Teaching your cluttering children to revere clear space as well as the orderly arrangement of things will help them not clutter as adults. We cluttering adults feel we have to fill every available space with something in order to feel comfortable. Only after we've recovered a bit, do we assign value to clear space.

## Prioritizing and Making Decisions

Boy, this is a tough one for everyone—adults and kids. For those who naturally clutter, it's the hardest thing to learn, but it's the key to doing just about everything. One trick that works pretty well for most kids is to make charts on different colors of poster paper for different subjects. Red could be History, blue could be Math (we don't want them to get into the habit of using red ink for Math, do we?), and so on. Make the poster large enough to encompass a month, so that long-term projects can go on it.

Every day, have them write down what homework or reading they have to do in each subject. Write in the due dates of the long-term projects a few days before they're actually due. This gives them a finish line (I don't like the word "deadline"—too negative), yet provides some wiggle room. I know, some people will say that the kids will compensate. Just like using "about time," the secret is to use an arbitrary number of days for each project's finish line. It could be one, five, three, or whatever strikes them at the moment. Don't forget to have a poster with scheduled activities such as band practice, sports games, and so on. This will help them realize that nothing exists in a vacuum. Everything is related to something else. We have a finite number of hours, thus a finite number of things we can accomplish.

The schedule will be more real to them if they can check off or put a big X in each square as they finish a project. Think of it as an adult's to-do list. I like the term "doing list," as it implies more continuous action, but I don't think it'll catch on. Don't you get a thrill scratching through something you've done?

The decision-making part comes when they have to decide on their own which project to tackle first. What materials do they need to get each assignment done? Can they prepare these in advance to make it easier in the long run?

## Breaking Things Into Manageable Components

Everyone's natural tendency is to start with the easiest task and put off the hard ones. The chart makes it obvious what has to be done when. Help kids understand that doing a little bit of the hard ones every day keeps them from being so intimidating.

If they've got 10 chapters to read in History, a paper to write for English, and 12 problems to solve in Math, it'll seem overwhelming. If they can figure out what to do, piece by piece, it can all get done. But just like decluttering, if they lump it all into the category of "homework I'll never get done," they'll just get overwhelmed.

You'll probably have to intervene at first, to teach them the habit of breaking things down. Relate it to how they cleaned up their rooms.

Each subject is a room and each bit of homework is a zone. (Remember the laser beams?) Those 10 intimidating chapters are just so many paragraphs or pages. Help them choose to read X number of pages each day, with a day for reviewing. Encourage them to take notes, either on the computer or in a notebook. This break from the activity of reading helps reinforce what they've learned and gives them a change from the chore of reading.

Math problems build on each other. If the problem is too daunting, help them understand that they can go back to the building block and start from there. It's just in a different zone that's already been put away.

## Keeping Notes Together

"I've found that the kids who have one notebook with several dividers do better with less stress than those who have five different notebooks to carry around."

—David,
an elementary school teacher

Kids lose things. Clutterers can't find things. With kid clutterers, you've got a recipe for disaster if they have several notebooks. In today's world, with so much being done on the computer, it's a good idea to have a three-ring binder for the notebook. That way, your kids can put the papers and notes they've taken on their computers into the main school notebook. That keeps like things with like.

"Young kids don't know how to keep a notebook or put things in folders."

—Karen Wiggins, Ph.D.,
school counselor

This is an area where parents can help a lot. Take the time to explain to your kids what a notebook is and show them how to use it. You might use your own date book or organizer to show them that even adults need a little help to keep track of things. If your organizer is held together with overworked rubber bands straining to contain unruly papers trying to make a break for it, you might want to neaten it up, even if only temporarily, before using it for show-and-tell.

## Consequences

> "Kids with disorganized lockers are late for class. Sometimes they have to suffer the consequences of being disorganized."
>
> —Karen Wiggins, Ph.D.,
> school counselor

Kids made mistakes, just like adults. Mistakes are good. We learn more from them than we do from effortlessly doing everything right. If one child is constantly late because she didn't put her schoolwork together the night before, don't penalize yourself and the other kids by sacrificing your routine for her tardiness. If she has to go to school without books or assignments once or twice, chances are she won't do it again. If she gets reprimanded for consistently being late for class, ask her to see if she can figure out why she's always late.

If she doesn't come up with the obvious, but a set of excuses instead, "Kids are always talking to me and that makes me late," for instance, teach her that she can explain to others that she has to be somewhere and suggest they talk later. Learning to say no is hard for clutterers. So is blaming others.

If she says something such as, "It's those dumb lockers at school. They aren't big enough," you're really onto something. Most likely, according to teachers, a kid's tardiness is due to her locker being disorganized. Cluttered kids spend more time rooting through things when they switch from one class to the next. It could be just that she doesn't know how to organize her locker. I don't recall any classes such as "Locker Organization 101." Set up an example at home of what her school locker is like and practice establishing some organizing principles.

### Unlock the Stress in Lockers

The above scenario could have a different and even simpler explanation. Maybe your kid just doesn't know how to operate her lock.

"In middle school we have combination locks on the lockers. We spend a lot of time teaching sixth graders how to open a lock. Parents could teach them that at home and make their lives easier. Children with disabilities often can't use a combination lock, so ask the school to let them use a key lock."

—Karen Wiggins, Ph.D.,
school counselor

Get a combination lock and have a few practice runs at working it before your children trot off to schools with lockers. I wish my parents had done this. Because of the constant stress of not being able to open my locker, I developed a real dislike for combination locks. Seriously. Maybe it has something to do with being left-handed, but it always took me several tries to get the darned thing open. I think my first curse words were aimed at a combination lock. I couldn't practice with it because it was at school and we didn't have any at home. (Maybe my parents feared them too?) I was too embarrassed to ask my folks to get me one to work with at home. After all, I was supposed to be a genius. Your kids may be too embarrassed to ask you too.

### Time Awareness

"During my first three years in grade school, I was the slowpoke of the family. My three sisters and one brother were the "good" ones. They ate, dressed, and made it to the car so that my father could take them to school. I was the "bad" one, who'd be upstairs, fighting a losing battle, desperately searching for some item I couldn't find, like the mate to my other shoe. With long and drawn out syllables, my name would float up the staircase. The voice belonged to one of my sisters, and had an impatient and angry tone. I knew I was keeping everyone waiting. My stomach in knots, I'd continue to struggle until, finally, I'd be ready. Instead of showing up triumphantly, I'd slink into the backseat of the car in the manor of a guilty dog, averting others' gazes, my tail between my legs.

"During my fourth year of grade school, we attended a different school, one that was within walking distance. We each prepared for school at our own pace. I could wait till the last minute and not feel guilty about stealing others' time. (I had the freedom to make only myself miserable!) I carried this habit all the way up through the grades, and on into my adult life."

—Tyrone,
a recovering clutterer

Clutterers don't grasp the concept of time very well. It's like we relate to time in another way than normal people. The earlier example of getting kids cool-looking watches can help. They can set alarms on them and their cell phones, if they have them. But, depending on ringing, having a beeping machine is not becoming aware of time. That takes mindfulness. Try having your kids sit quietly in a room without clocks, computers, or other visual time clues such as radios and microwave ovens that have clocks. Hardly anyone sets them, but they can clue someone in to the passage of time. Whether it's 8:27 a.m. or 8:27 p.m., 10 minutes is 10 minutes.

Make it a game, especially if you have multiple darlings. Have them guess when 10 minutes have passed (for younger ones that will be an eternity, so make it 5). Do this a few times until a pattern emerges. Then, if they are consistently over or under the number of minutes, they can apply that to their breaks between classes. Of course, schools have clocks they could look at if they really wanted to be on time, but it's good training to learn how to use our inner clock.

## Night Owls or Day People?

As a practicing night owl, I'm a firm believer in giving all people as much control over when they want to do things as possible. Kids in school still need to get to bed way early by adult standards, but if one kid is a night person and the other a day person, maybe they could do their homework at different times. When I was a kid, during summer vacation, I spent hours on the roof pulling in shortwave stations on my radio. Parents' big fear today is that if their kids are away after 10:00 or midnight (or whatever curfew is in your house), they're up to no good. They probably are. Nighttime does seem to lower inhibitions. But if they're at home, they could be putting their productive hours to good use. Unfortunately, most of us have to fit into the world of day people, but let your kids determine what time they learn best. By the way, adult clutterers are predominately night owls.

## The Bottom Line

How well your children do in school depends on a lot of factors, and cluttering or being disorganized isn't the only one. If they do well in one or two subjects and not in others, it could be that they just have a natural affinity for those subjects and are willing to put in the effort to be organized enough to do what it takes to excel in them. Remember the comments of Mr. Montgomery, the bandmaster? You may be able to help them apply those techniques to other subjects, but if they don't want to, they don't want to. That's got nothing to do with their cluttering and is outside the scope of this book. All I can say is that organization can only do so much. If they can use it when they want, they've got the skills. Desire is more important than skill.

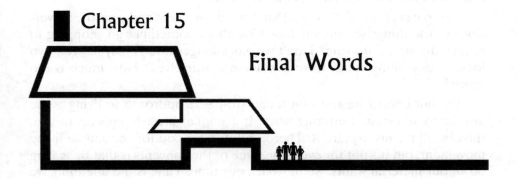

# Chapter 15

# Final Words

> *My wife and I work hard and long hours so that I*
> *can provide a better standard of living for my*
> *children than I had growing up. But sometimes I*
> *wonder if it's worth it. Am I working at a job I don't*
> *like and missing seeing my kids grow up just so they*
> *can get the next Xbox, or more clothes they wear*
> *once and then lose in their already overstuffed*
> *closet?*
>
> —Bill G.

We're at the end of our visit together. Thank you for inviting me into your homes, your lives. By now, you have the tools and understanding you need to help yourself and your children learn to live clutter-free lives. These last thoughts of mine are more philosophical in nature than how-to. Philosophy is how we shape our unconscious attitudes about how we live.

Essential to not-cluttering is not-buying. I'm not a minimalist. Things aren't bad. Having too many things just gets in the way of living. Everything has a price—not just what it costs, but in maintenance and the time and space it takes up.

Madison Avenue knows how big a market kids represent. So do you. Each year there's a new, hot toy, game, or clothing style. Your kids just won't be happy until they have it. Or will they? Do they really need more stuff? Can you convince them that getting each new highly touted product that comes down the pike isn't going to make them happy? Can you not convince them and still have peace in the family?

Are parents any different? Don't we want "new and improved" versions of the things we already have? Don't we sometimes go shopping to relieve the stress of living? Don't we work longer hours, maybe even two jobs, to buy more things for our kids—and ourselves? How much is too much?

I'm not one to suggest that a back-to-basics approach to living is the answer to all of our cluttering woes. If a simpler lifestyle appeals to you, then by all means explore it. There's a lot to be said for the simple living movement, but it's not for everyone. One of the concepts is that by scaling down our material wants, we buy back our time. Time is the one thing we cannot buy. To a certain extent, we can buy health. We can purchase the right foods and dietary supplements. We buy health insurance so we can get checkups and medical care when it's needed. But even with health, there's a component we cannot buy. We need time to exercise—a big part of staying healthy. So we're back to time again. And we need time to chill out, to recharge our batteries for our mental health.

There's nothing wrong with stuff. We need a certain amount of stuff to live, and more to make our lives easier and more interesting. Children need toys and games to stimulate their minds, to develop motor skills, and to learn how to share and interact with other children. Unless you live on a farm, the likelihood of your children finding their amusement by unrestricted roaming about in nature is slim. For most of us, even a trip to "nature" involves cars, camping gear, special clothing, and more stuff. Getting back to nature has become structured.

## Replace *Getting* With *Giving*

If you can teach your children that giving things they don't use to others feels even better than buying new stuff, you've achieved something worthwhile. Schools and churches have clothing drives, Christmas drives, and organized events to give back to the community. Not only can your children give their discarded items, they can give their time to help these causes.

Sadly, we live in a culture that has too many things. Major thrift stores routinely discard items that are given to them because they don't have the space to store them.

There are smaller charities that don't get enough donations of things, and giving to them is more likely to help the ones who need it. Women's shelters need lots of kid stuff. The Salvation Army does a good job of distributing discards. Animal shelters constantly need old clothes, sheets, bedspreads. You probably know families who are struggling financially. I can't think of a better way to get rid of things than direct donations.

Churches take groups of children and adults to foreign countries to build homes for people who have none. They take lots of items with them to give away. Encourage your kids to participate. This way, they'll get to see how their gifts can dramatically change the lives of those less fortunate.

Having fewer things doesn't necessarily equate with being less as people. Many of the greatest people in the world grew up with few material possessions. Survivors of the Holocaust came through their ordeal with only their lives. Emigrants, through the ages, have come to our shores with nothing. What these people brought to us and to our culture was an understanding that the human spirit is what is truly important. If you teach your children that who they are has nothing to do with what they have, you will have raised model citizens.

## Hope for the Cluttered

I sincerely hope you've gotten a lot of good out of this book. I hope that it has opened your eyes to ways of changing your children's and your own cluttering behavior. I hope that you've come to understand that kids and adults hold onto things for reasons that have nothing to do with the intrinsic value of the things themselves. Cluttering is an emotional reaction to something else. If we learn to deal with the emotional aspect, we can eliminate the physical possessions.

Reading this book, by itself, will not declutter your life. It will take both applying the principles herein presented and understanding what's behind the clutter. It will take work. It will take constant vigilance. Clutter is part of living. Stuff keeps coming into our lives. Once we decide that we aren't gong to let stuff steal our lives and our time, we can stem the flow. Clutter can wreck families. But learning to not-clutter and declutter as a family can put them back together again. And that, my friends, is what I hope you do.

The following is from *Plato's Dialogues*, from Socrates' conversation with Phaedrus from the Third Jowett Translation, Liveright Publishing Corp., 1954:

> SOCRATES: ... give me beauty in the inward soul; and may the outward and inward man be at one. May I reckon the wise to be the wealthy, and may I have such a quantity of gold as a temperate man and he only can bear and carry.
>
> Anything more? The prayer, I think is enough for me.
>
> PHAEDRUS: Ask the same for me, for friends should have all things in common.
>
> SOCRATES: Let us go.

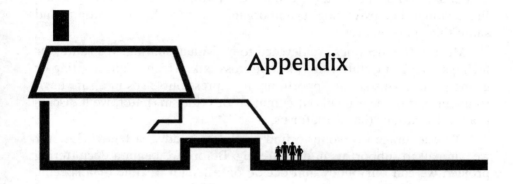

# Appendix

## Clutterless Recovery Groups Statement of Principles

We are a peer-based, self-help group for people who have a problem with clutter in their lives: physical, emotional, spiritual. Decluttering our lives is more than cleaning out junk. It is clearing our spirits. We didn't get this way overnight and we won't get where we want to be in one meeting. That's why we keep coming back to meetings. Our progress will wax and wane, but we never give up. We build clutter-free lives on a series of small successes—one bit of clutter at a time.

If your own disorderliness or clutter, or that of a family member is causing distress, you'll find solutions that work for real clutterers here. Whether you are only a little disorganized, a hoarder, have AD/HD, or are just overwhelmed by your clutter, you're in the right place.

We often believe that we don't deserve more in our lives, so we hang onto items and papers we no longer need. We may fear we will never have enough or know everything. We learn to trust ourselves that we can discard those things that do not serve us anymore. We learn to trust ourselves to make decisions. We are successful. We are powerful. We are free.

We have no specific religious or other affiliations. We are not a 12-Step Program. We are equals who learn decluttering tools so that we can live successful, happy lives. We respect the privacy of all who share. What you say here stays here.

We leave all decisions about therapy to the individual. We do not take the place of therapists and have no opinions on treatments or medications. Our goal is to help each other, as only peers with the same challenges can. Professionals like psychologists and organizers are welcome to attend and share their perspectives.

Most of the meetings are devoted to individual sharing. We share our feelings about our cluttering, without cross talk, which is interrupting or giving advice. This is our opportunity to express ourselves in a safe environment and be heard without comment or criticism. Later, we'll discuss practical solutions that work for us.

We encourage everyone to find a "clutter-buddy," a fellow clutterer we can call to support us in decluttering. Before we begin a decluttering project, we call our buddy and decide on a length of time or a specific project to tackle. We commit to calling our buddy back to share our progress. If we are stuck, we discuss it. Even if we don't achieve our goal, we are successful, because we faced our clutter. Buddies might be invited to our homes or offices to physically help, if we so choose.

We are all expressions of God's love, and He wants us all to live happy, joyful, orderly lives. We are successful and perfect in our own way. We help each other realize this. Our success and self-worth do not come from people, places, or things. They are outward expressions of our inner perfection. We seek to help each other unlock that expression. Please join us at *www.clutterless.org* for support.

## Promises for Clutterers

- We will know more happiness and freedom from worry.

- We will know the joy of not having to hide our shame.

- We will feel more self-confident and secure.

- We will feel like a whole new world has opened up to us.

- We will stop our negative self-talk about our cluttering..

- We will stop blaming others for what is our responsibility.

- We will stop being afraid of having people know the real us.

- We will develop a more spiritual manner of living, which will help us in all areas of our lives.

- We will share our experiences with others, to help them and us.

- We will accept our imperfections as expressions of our humanity.

- Our relationships will improve as the stress of our cluttering lessens.

- We will be more successful because we have eliminated our self-sabotaging tendencies.

- We will no longer live in a fog of mental confusion.

- We will no longer procrastinate.

- We will experience peace and joy in all areas of our lives.

- We will no longer feel overwhelmed by our clutter.

- We will accept our Shadow Self as part of us, but not let it define us.

- We will live in light and beauty in all ways.

- We will be free to love and let ourselves be loved.

- We will accept the unlimited good that flows into our lives as we make room for it by eliminating our clutter.

## Affirmations for Clutterers

- I live in a clutter-free environment—mentally, spiritually, emotionally.

- I see beyond my clutter. I see the orderliness that lies within.

- My life is filled with beauty and organization.

- I am a perfect expression of universal love.

- I allow myself to be imperfect in the eyes of others, knowing I am a perfect me.

- Clutter is the past. Order is the present. Peace and prosperity are the future.

- I start my day over whenever I need to.

- God doesn't make junk. I do. With His help, we can eliminate it.

- No task is overwhelming to me. I have the strength to overcome every limitation.

- My finances are in perfect order.

- There is always enough money in the universe for my every need. I now claim my fair share.

- Oops! I had a slip. It is not serious. If I can do it, I can undo it.

- Time is a precious gift. I do not waste it on people, places, or things that do not contribute to my growth.

- Thank you, Great Spirit, for the prosperity that right now flows to me as the rivers flow to the ocean and the ocean flows back to the shore.

- The longest journey begins with the first step. I confidently take that step, knowing that I am guided in the right direction.

- There is plenty in this world for me. I lovingly release those items that are no longer useful, knowing in truth that whatever I need has already been provided.

- Money flows into my life according to the space I allow it.

- GOD—Good Orderly Direction, is my guide on this journey to orderliness.

- Clean, clean, clean! That is my house!

- Neat, neat, neat! That is my life!

- As I clear my physical clutter, I clear my mental and emotional clutter. My life is clutter-free on all levels.

See Resources section for address and contact information.

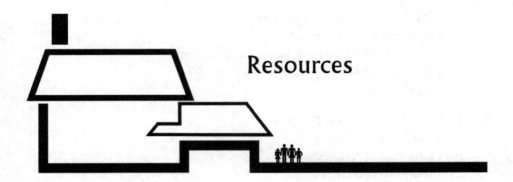

# Resources

## Websites and Discussion Groups

*add.miningco.com/gi/dynamic/offsite.htm?site=http://www.addhelpline.org*—Eileen Bailey's ADD support site.

*add.miningco.com/library/blsupportmain.htm*—Links to support groups in general, including AD/HD for kids and adults.

*groups.msn.com/MomsofADHDKids/_homepage.msnw?pgmarket=en-us*—A Yahoo group for moms of kids with AD/HD.

*groups.yahoo.com/group/clutterfree*—Interesting discussion group for clutterers, with a psychological focus.

*www.aacap.org*—The American Academy of Child & Adolescent Psychology. Expert professional information on every aspect of child psychology.

*www.clutterless.org*—Discussion group and online chat run by clutterers and the author.

*www.homeschoolzone.com/add/index.htm*—Several online discussion groups about homeschooling and parenting in general.

*www.mentalhealth.com*—An excellent site for professionally written and researched mental health information of all kinds.

## Organizations

**Attention Deficit Disorder Association (ADDA)**
>1788 Second Street, Suite 200
>Highland Park, IL 60035
>Phone: 847-432-ADDA (to leave a message)
>Fax: 847-432-5874   *484- 945- 2101*
>*www.add.org*

**Clutterless Recovery Groups, Inc.**
>1714 54th Street, Ste. B
>Galveston, TX 77551-4717
>Phone: 409-744-1289
>*www.clutterless.org*

For an information kit on what they do and how to start a meeting in your town, send a ruquest with a return envelope (9 x 12-inch with $.83 postage) to the address provided. A $5 donation is appreciated to defray expenses.

**Parents Without Partners, Inc.**
>*www.parentswithoutpartners.org*

International support group for single parents. Provides meetings, discussion groups, speakers, study groups, and publications geared to the challenges and solutions of single-parent families.

**Alternatives for Simple Living**
>*www.simpleliving.org*

A socially and environmentally aware nonprofit group, started in 1973, that "equips people of faith to challenge consumerism, live justly and celebrate responsibly."

**Simple Living Network**
>*www.simpleliving.net*

Collection of people who have sought out a simpler, less material- istic way of life. Discussion groups nationwide.

## Licensed Professional Counselors Specializing in ADD or AD/HD Adults

**Wilma Fellman, M.Ed., LPC**

> E-mail: WRZF@aol.com

> Wilma Fellman is a Career and Life Planning Counselor specializing in working with ADD or AD/HD adults in Michigan. She is also "an adult with ADD, a parent with ADD, and the mother of the former poster child for ADD."

## Family Counselors

**Karen Griggs, MFT**

> Email: pgriggs@pacbell.com
> Phone: 818-761-5855.

> Karen Griggs is a Marriage and Family Counselor in Burbank, California.

## Professional Organizers

**Jan Jasper**

> E-mail: jan@janjasper.com
> Phone: 212-465-7472 or 718-435-3199
> Fax: 509-356-2803
> *www.janjasper.com*

> Jan Jasper is a New York City productivity and time-management consultant and highly recommended.

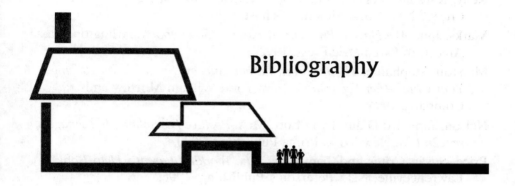

# Bibliography

Barkley, Russell A., Ph.D. *Taking Charge of ADHD: The Complete, Authoritative Guide for Parents*. New York: The Guilford Press, 1995.

Bradley, Michael J., Ed.D. *Yes, Your Parents Are Crazy*. Gig Harbor, Wash.: Harbor Press, 2004.

———. *Yes, Your Teen Is Crazy!: Loving Your Kid Without Losing Your Mind*. Gig Harbor, Wash.: Harbor Press, 2002.

Coren, Stanley. *The Left-Hander Syndrome*. New York: Vintage Books, 1993.

Faber, Adele and Elaine Mazlish. *How to Talk So Kids Will Listen & Listen So Kids Will Talk*. New York: Avon Books, 1999.

Fellman, Wilma R., M.Ed., LPC and Arnold C. *The Other Me: Poetic Thoughts on ADD for Adults, Kids and Parents*. Plantation Fla.: Specialty Press, 1997.

Hallowell, Edward M., M.D. *Driven to Distraction*. New York: Touchstone Books, 1995.

Ingersoll, Barbara D., PhD., and Sam Goldstein, Ph.D. *Lonely, Sad and Angry: A Parent's Guide to Depression in Children and Adolescents*. New York: Doubleday, 1995.

Jowett. Benjamin E., trans. *The Dialogues of Plato*. New York: Liveright Publishing Corp., 1954.

Kabat-Zinn, Myla and Jon. *Everyday Blessings: The Inner Work of Mindful Parenting.* New York: Hyperion Press, 1997.

Kelly, Kate and Peggy Ramundo. *You Mean I'm Not Lazy, Stupid or Crazy?!* New York: Simon & Schuster, 1996.

Marks, Jane. *We Have a Problem: A Parent's Sourcebook.* Arlington, Va.: American Psychiatric Press, 1992.

Marston, Stephanie. *The Divorced Parent: Success Strategies for Raising Your Child After Separation.* New York: William Morrow and Company, 1994.

Nelson, Jane, Ed.D and Lynn Lott, M.A. *Positive Discipline for Teenagers, rev. 2nd ed.* New York: Prima Publishing, 2000.

Price, Susan Crites and Tom Price. *The Working Parent's Help Book.* Lawrenceville, N.J.: Peterson's Publishing, 1996.

Rosenfeld, Alvin M.D. and Nicole Wise. *Hyper-Parenting: Are You Hurting Your Child by Trying Too Hard?* New York: St. Martin's Press, 2000.

————. *The Over-Scheduled Child: Avoiding the Hyper-Parenting Trap.* New York: St. Martin's Press, 2001.

Silver, Larry B., M.D. *Dr. Larry Silver's Advice to Parents on ADHD, 2nd ed.* New York: Times Books (Random House), 1995.

Spock, Benjamin, M.D. *Dr. Spock's Baby and Child Car, 7th ed.* New York: Dutton Books, an imprint of the Penguin Group, 1998.

Zweig, Connie and Jeremiah Abrams, eds. *Meeting the Shadow: The Hidden Power of the Dark Side of Human Nature.* New York: Jeremy P. Tarcher, Inc., 1991.

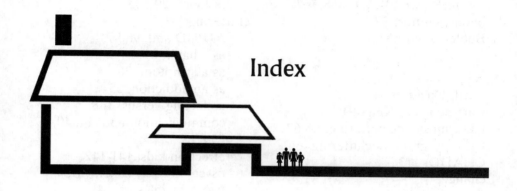

# Index

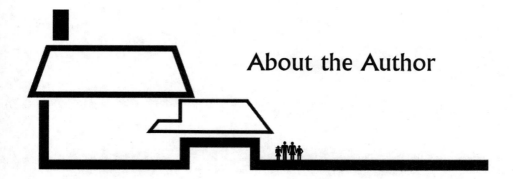

# About the Author

MIKE NELSON has worked with hundreds of clutterers and families since founding Clutterless Recovery Groups, Inc. in 2000. He's worked with children and teens as a Sunday School teacher, and in the areas of drug and alcohol abuse. In the writing of this book, he consulted with dozens of parents, teens, and children, as well as teachers and psychiatric profession-als specializing in child and family behavior. This is his third book on clut-tering as psychological, emotional, and spiritual blockages. As a reformed clutterer himself (he's eliminated more than a ton of no-longer-needed items from his life), he understands that helping people understand why they clutter is more important than telling them that simple rules and sys-tems will solve their cluttering challenges. Working from the inside out has more lasting effects than concentrating on the stuff itself.

He's been a guest of the Dr. Laura Schlessinger Show, the American Association of Retired Persons (AARP), and Associated Press news shows, as well as radio and TV stations across the country. He's been profiled for his work with clutterers by *The Los Angeles Times, CNN, Houston Chronicle, Galveston Daily News* and has been quoted for his unique perspective by *The Motley Fool*, and *Atlantic Monthly*.

Nelson has lectured on cluttering from a psychological perspective to civic, business, and church groups nationally, and presents workshops coast to coast. You can hear audio and video clips of his speaking at *www.clutterless.org*.

He lives on Galveston Island, Texas, and has published 17 books.